Be Alive in Christ

Youth Group Strategies

Be Alive in Christ

Robert Doolittle

Saint Mary's Press
Christian Brothers Publications
Winona, Minnesota

Thank you, Arthur, Jim, Carol, Ed, Ron, Carol, and Pat, for a vision of parish that calls all generations to walk with Jesus.

Thank you, Pete Moloney, for your dream of reaching our teens and for building a youth board to make it happen.

Thank you, *Pilot,* for publishing the youth ministry columns that gave this book its start.

Thank you, Simon Harak, for all the editing help you gave me on those early columns.

Thank you, Sister Dolora, for the constant encouragement to keep writing.

Thank you, Katherine, for all that typing and for the times you wouldn't let me get away with sections that needed to be rethought and rewritten.

Thank you, Bob Stamschror, for the patient and affirming way you worked with me and turned my straw into well-edited gold.

And thank you to all who have permitted the stories of your teenage spiritual adventures to provide the rich layer of truth on which this book totally depends.

The publishing team included Robert P. Stamschror, development editor; Rebecca L. Fairbank, manuscript editor; Gary J. Boisvert, typesetter; Carolyn St. George, cover designer, cover artist, and illustrator; Jack B. Huhnerkoch, cover photo; pre-press, printing, and binding by the graphics division of Saint Mary's Press.

The acknowledgments continue on page 188.

Printed in the United States of America

Printing: 6 5 4 3 2 1

Year: 1996 95 94 93 92 91

ISBN 0-88489-246-8

I dedicate this book to two families:

- *to my wife, Katherine, and my three children, Kate, Simon, and Andrew, who gave me the space and the confidence to write*
- *to my Saint Agnes family, who gave me the best job I can imagine—sharing Christ with young people*

Contents

Foreword

Bob Doolittle has spent over fifteen years living and working out the hows and whys of the Catholic youth ministry model that is portrayed in this book. Along the way, he has placed what he has come to know before the Lord Jesus in prayer and before the ministering parish in which he works. Now he places his experiences and knowledge before you.

You will find here an array of programming ideas (not "fun-first" ideas but "fun-too" ideas) that celebrate life's goodness with the enthusiasm of young people and confront life's struggles with the passionate intensity of young people. The range of strategies encompasses exuberant dances, liturgies with maximum involvement, healing and guidance experiences, searching explorations of teen issues, and outreach to people in need.

Integrated into these strategies for youth ministry is an essential and often omitted ingredient for effective parish youth work—the ingredient of *evangelization*—which involves offering the young people opportunities to meet and actively respond to the person, message, and church of Jesus Christ.

Young people are growing up in youth cultures and adult societies that are, in effect, post-Christian—that is, societies becoming daily more secularized and materialistic. Today's young people are in great need of, and are surprisingly ready for, evangelization—in many instances "explicit" evangelization. They need a pastoral approach to youth ministry that brings the Good News of Jesus into their daily choices and relationships. As Pope John Paul II said in his 1979 address to young people in Mexico:

> With the vivacity that is characteristic of your age, with the generous enthusiasm of your young hearts, walk towards Christ. He alone is the solution to all your problems. He alone is the way, the truth, and the life; He alone is the real salvation of the world; He alone is the hope of mankind. . . . Let it be your commitment and your program to love Jesus, with a sincere, authentic, and personal love. He must be your commitment and your friend and your support along the path of life. He alone has words of eternal life. (*Allow Him to Find You* [Washington, DC: Catholic University of America, 1979], p. 12)

Today's young people need explicit evangelization, but we often do not know how to evangelize authentically or, at the same time, how to make evangelization's worth and value so real to the young that they grab onto it as essential for their life. *Be Alive in Christ* is rich in this kind of know-how.

Yet, from another perspective, perhaps this book's greatest value is that it provides youth ministers a way to nudge parish leaders and members into greater comfort with evangelization of young people—that is, with explicit evangelization as the center of their pastoral vision of youth ministry. Such a pastoral vision, when held and supported alike by youth ministers, priests, other parish leaders, and the parish community-at-large, can give new life and energy to a parish's efforts to reach its young people.

Fr. Ed Malone
Our Lady of Grace Parish
Chelsea, Massachusetts

Introduction

This book has two parts. Part A focuses on helping our young people become *fully alive as human persons.* Part B is about helping them become *close to the person of Christ.* One premise unites both parts of the book:

> Being fully alive
> is only possible
> close to Christ.

This is not fundamentalism. Christ comes to us in many ways, not all of them under his own name. But he does come, offering new life not only to young people but to everyone. Here is how I often express Christ's Gospel purpose to young Catholics:

> Christ wants to free
> the person you carry
> hidden within you.
> If you will let him,
> he will come and

help you bring out fully
the human being
you were conceived and born to be.

Part A of this book, "Freeing the Human," centers on the young people's beautiful but often terribly embattled humanity and proposes many ways to encourage them to believe and have confidence in their amazing possibilities as human persons.

Part B, "Inviting the Divine," focuses on the great friend the young people have in Christ and proposes many ways they can meet him, hear him, trust him, and follow him into fullness of life.

The theology underlying both parts of the book is the following:

> The transforming work of God in young lives can take place only when there is an opened-up "I" and an opened-up "Thou." As youth ministers, we can help that struggling young "I" to find itself and to find expression. And we can help the young people to get in touch with that loving, divine "Thou" as well.

The first part of this book builds up the "I" side of the "I-Thou" relationship; the second part builds up the "Thou" side. Both parts present a full set of strategies in the context of true stories that illustrate how each strategy works. The strategies in part A reach in toward the emerging young person. The strategies in part B reach out toward Christ, their great friend.

This book proposes a ministry that shuttles back and forth between an intense humanism and an intense mysticism. Here's how I like to challenge young people to go beyond the barriers they might have in either direction:

> The more real
> you are with Christ,
> the more real
> he will be for you.
> And the reverse
> is equally true.

My bias—and my experience with adolescents—is that the human is naturally mystical. The natural and the mystical belong to each other as two parts of a whole, mutually enriching and nurturing each other, producing a wonderful aliveness and maturity in a person that neither could bring about by itself.

Helping young people become alive in Christ is the purpose of this book, and it is the ultimate gift we can give to them. But this book is not just about teenagers becoming alive in Christ. It is also about us as youth ministers becoming alive in Christ along with the young people we serve.

In John 10:10, Jesus sums up his empowering mission to every person, young and old alike: "'I have come that they may have life, and have it to the full'" (NIV).

Part A
Freeing
the Human

In 1976, *A Vision of Youth Ministry* was published by the United States Catholic Conference (USCC), and Catholic youth work has not been the same since. With prophetic boldness, the vision paper called the Catholic church in the United States to generate parish programs that "foster the total personal and spiritual growth of each young person" (Washington, DC: USCC, p. 7).

The chapters in part A of this book cover the story of our parish's response to the inspiring call of that vision paper. Our theological premise is this:

> In his own person, the Jesus we see moving through the Gospels presents a double revelation. In him we discover what God is like, and we also discover what the fully realized human person is like. Jesus opens our eyes to the depths of the human as well as to the heights of the Divine.

Our young people, with so many forces working against them, especially need this freeing revelation of their human potential. They need to hear us say with Jesus, "Come on, don't be afraid. Be the person you are. Don't let anything stop you." But before young people can hear that "good news" from us, they first need *us* to hear *their* news—the news of their own human struggle to live fully.

Young people have much anguish to share with us—and much joy, many frustrations, and many ideas. When we have listened long enough and deeply enough so that they know they have been heard, then they in turn need to hear the liberating Good News of Christ as it comes from our own stories, from the Gospels, and from the church that loves them. Young people need to hear from us a word that opens their eyes and strengthens their heart.

Each chapter in this part of the book, therefore, attends to something specific that young people are feeling, thinking, doing, or needing, and each chapter proposes strategies to generate honest dialog about that particular issue—an encounter between their news and the Good News of Christ. Each chapter begins by addressing a specific challenge that young people face. Then, in the context of open and trusting relationships, some specific ways of coaching them to handle the challenge are offered. The coaching is Gospel-oriented, and it will empower the young people to come through their struggles *more* alive and capable than before, not less.

For many young people in our groups, the sheer size of the challenges they face would quite readily knock the courage and the faith right out of them if the Good News were not made accessible through us. The young people's wholeness is at stake, and much depends on what they find in us and in the ministry that we offer.

The very urgency of the young people's needs can make us preachy and pushy. Or, as a backlash from that extreme, we can back into another extreme and become tentative—afraid to do any clear coaching. But Jesus is neither pushy nor tentative. He listens carefully. He speaks clearly. And so must we.

If our young people are to be healthy, feisty, free, and courageous—like Jesus—our ministry style must be like that too. The stories, passages, principles, and strategies offered here are meant to encourage you to minister with the boldness and joy of Christ's own Spirit. When the young people find Jesus through what we say and do, our ministry will have that special dynamism that enables his promise of abundant life to be true for them and to come true in them.

1
Icebreakers:
Building Trust Through Laughter

Lyman Coleman, widely regarded as *the* authority on Christian group dynamics, prescribes laughter for any group that wants to do some serious sharing. Once, at a Serendipity Workshop, he said that we are never more open to the Holy Spirit than when we are laughing.

Everyone faced with meeting a new group of people is held back by a secret fear of looking ridiculous. So Coleman's approach is to begin a sharing session by asking people to say or do some pretty ridiculous things in order to dissolve their fear into shared laughter. Then it becomes a lot safer for people to be themselves with the group, because they have all just shared a common baptism of laughter.

A good speaker is playful with an audience early on—maybe by telling a joke or by making some offhand remarks—to relax the audience and establish good rapport. A good group leader really has to do the same thing. But because a leader wants everyone in the group to do some speaking, he or she must provide a way for everyone to become playful and relaxed with everyone else. Therefore, a youth minister should always keep handy a bagful of laughter-inducing icebreakers and should use them generously at meetings, workshops, or conferences—in any and every setting where young people are being invited to do some sharing and learning together.

The icebreakers described in this chapter and the games described in chapter 2 have one important element in common—they often involve a lot of good, healthy touching. In chapter 6, I mention the vital importance of appropriate physical contact for healthy personal development. Being comfortable with appropriate touching will be helpful, if not essential, for successfully directing both the icebreakers and the games that I describe.

On the other hand, games and icebreakers have two very distinct uses. Icebreakers take up little time or space and can easily be tucked in before more substantial program offerings as hors d'oeuvres to whet the appetite for lively involvement. Games entail more time, space, and preparation; are a lot more active than icebreakers; and are most useful for parties, picnics, and other social celebrations.

The five icebreakers that follow have worked well for our youth group in a variety of situations. The first is one that we created ourselves.

1. The Ezekiel Wheels

Our group leaders made up this icebreaker for a meeting when a lot of new people were coming into a well-established group. We wanted people to form new ties and to be comfortable enough to discuss their efforts to live as Christians.

Introduce the activity by explaining to the group that they are about to put into practice a fairly unusual interpretation of Ezekiel's first vision, in which he sees a wheel within a wheel.

To begin the game, tell the group members to pair off with someone whom they don't know very well. Then ask the group members to form two circles (or wheels), one inside the other. One partner should stand in the inside circle facing out, and the other partner should stand in the outside circle facing in.

When both of the circles have been formed, give the group these instructions:

> When I say go, the two circles will rotate in opposite directions and come to a complete stop at the seventh person. As you pass the six other people, pause, shake hands, and say something brief but friendly to each one.

Sit down when you reach person number seven. Ready, set, go!

Sit back, watch the joyful pandemonium, and wait until the new pairs are all seated nose-to-nose. Tell the group that Ezekiel would have been pleased with their wheels. Then give these directions:

Now you will discuss the questions I will give you with the person you are facing. Your questions for each other will come in pairs. The first question will be a ridiculous one, the second a serious one. The method to this madness is that when you've been ridiculous together, then you can more comfortably be serious together.

Explain to the group that they will have just three minutes each for the icebreaker questions and three minutes each for the soul-searching questions (but extend that limit if you sense that more time is needed). Give out the questions one pair at a time. Each new pair of questions signals a turning of the wheels, with a new handshake and hello to each person along the way.

Here are some sample questions that we concocted for our group:

1–a. What are you like when you first get up in the morning?

1–b. What person has most influenced your faith and how?

2–a. What were some of the goofy things that you did the first time you fell in love?

2–b. What do you like best about being a Catholic Christian? What do you like least?

3–a. What is your pet peeve (something that people do that really gets on your nerves)?

3–b. What has convinced you to believe in Jesus Christ and his message?

Feel free to change the order of the questions or the length of the list, depending on how the game is going. The playful questions and the serious questions have a reciprocal effect so the group can learn that laughter is important and deep dialog is fun.

The next four icebreakers are not originals, nor did we find them in books. So where did they come from? There is something like a youth ministry subculture in which all sorts of program ideas are circulated through contact among youth workers and their youth groups. That's how these four icebreakers came our way. I hope that your group will enjoy them as much as we have.

2. Shuffle Buns

Invite everyone to arrange their chairs in a circle and be seated. Then, working from a long homemade list, shout out something like "People with short tempers move five chairs to the left." The people that fit this description should immediately move to the left, making a little bounce-sit on each chair along the way, until they land at chair number five. It does not matter if that chair is already occupied—players may wind up on a lap or a pile of laps. When everyone is settled, shout out the next item: "People who think that the abbreviation Ms. is better than Miss or Mrs. move eight chairs to the left." Proceed through the list in this fashion.

Several young people can brainstorm a list of items in advance. (Once we made up the items as we went along. People just yelled them out one at a time, including simple stuff like "blue eyes" or "wearing red" and serious stuff like "ever thought of being a priest or some other type of church leader" or "got really angry with someone in the last two days.") A crazy mix of trivial and self-revealing items keeps everyone disclosing who they are as they bounce from chair to chair around the room.

3. "If You Love Me . . ."

Ask everyone to sit together in a circle. Begin with one person who will be the teaser. The teaser turns to the person next to her or him, the teasee, and tries to get a smile from the teasee by saying, "If you love me, won't you please, please smile?" The teasee must keep a straight face while responding, "You know that I love you, but I just can't smile." That dialog should be repeated three times. The teaser, while talking, can do just about anything (short of touching the teasee) to get her or him to smile. If the teaser succeeds in getting the teasee to smile, she or he wins. The teasee then becomes the teaser and turns to the person next to her or him and the sequence is repeated until everyone in the circle has been a teaser and a teasee. If the teaser does not get the teasee to smile by the third try, the teasee still becomes the next teaser.

Instead of playing the game in a circle, you can get serious and organize the game like a tournament that starts by pairing off the group members. Then winners play winners until you finally get an "if you love me" champion.

4. People Bingo

This icebreaker uses identity phrases just like the ones in "Shuffle Buns" except that the phrases are arranged on a sheet of twenty-five squares like a bingo card, five down and five

across, with a descriptive phrase in each square (except, of course, the center "free" square). Try items like these:
- good-looking but modest
- is carrying a rosary
- is madly in love with someone in this room
- has had a driver's license for less than six months

To play the game, everyone runs around the room trying to get signatures from people who will admit to one of the phrases on the card. The object is to fill a straight row with signatures, either vertically, horizontally, or diagonally. In five minutes you will probably have a roomful of people laughing, breathless, and well on their way to being comfortable with each other.

5. The Lap Circle

This is a quickie, and the fun of it lies in the group concentration and cooperation it requires. To begin, ask everyone to stand in a circle. The circle should be as perfectly round as possible. Then instruct everyone to turn to their right and, without losing that perfect roundness, inch sideways toward the center of the circle until everyone is snug up against the person in front of them and behind them. At the count of three, tell everyone to sit down (slowly if you're new at it, fast if you're brave) on the lap of the person behind them. The goal is an unbroken circle of occupied human chairs with nobody on the floor.

Youth groups have been doing this icebreaker for years. Supposedly, there is a world record of 1,468 people simultaneously and successfully sitting on each other's laps.

The icebreakers described in this chapter, and hundreds of others like them, can help generate an atmosphere of high energy in which people have a wonderful time exploring and sharing serious and personal topics.

A good way to keep freshening up your own repertoire of icebreaker ideas is to make a point of hobnobbing with other folks who do youth ministry. Also, you can buy them by the bookful from publishers like the following:

Abingdon Press
P.O. Box 801
201 Eighth Avenue South
Nashville, TN 37202
phone: 1-800-251-3320

Group Books
Box 48
Loveland, CO 80539
phone: 1-800-747-6060

Saint Mary's Press
702 Terrace Heights
Winona, MN 55987-1320
phone: 1-800-533-8095

Youth Specialties
1224 Greenfield Drive
El Cajon, CA 92021
phone: 1-800-253-1309

I'll close this chapter with a delightful story I once heard that helps make the case for including the merriment of icebreakers in youth ministry. The story is about the poet Emily Dickinson when she was a teenager in boarding school. Emily was reprimanded by the angry schoolmistress who had caught her skipping compulsory chapel: "And you probably haven't read your Bible either." She meant the daily required passage, but Emily misunderstood and answered, "Oh yes, Ma'am, I've read the Bible three times. The first time I found it a terrible bore. The second time I found it full of deep wisdom. But the third time I found it nearly merry."

The biblical word for this merriment of Emily's is *joy.* Gal. 5:22 names it as one of the fruits of the Spirit. Our word for it is *fun.* May the "spirit of fun" descend on our groups and permeate our spirituality, never to depart again.

2

Rowdy, Crazy Games: Playing Together at Church

"People drink for fun. Why would God be opposed to that?" Early in my work at Saint Agnes, I was being put on the spot by a frank group of young people who managed to keep one foot in the high school's fast lane and the other foot in the church. The question was an aggressive one, but a good one—voicing the usually unspoken rebellion of their generation. The young people were offering me both a challenge and a trust. They really wanted an answer.

I sidestepped the issue of whether drinking actually does produce any genuine fun and replied, "Because God has something much better to offer. Kingdom fun is more fun than drunken fun. As this community of ours gets rolling, you're going to find a better time here than at beer parties at the parks around town."

That particular group decided to stick around and try out my prediction that Kingdom fun is more fun than drunken fun, and in fact, they helped it come true. The point is a hard one to win though, and I find that lots of teens just will not buy it. They carry around a culturally acquired bias that cannot imagine all-out good times in church groups.

We continually have to hammer away at that bias, and that's where the rowdy, crazy games come in. These games firmly establish the element of uproarious play as appropriate in the life of the church.

I will repeat here what I said about icebreakers and games in chapter 1. Icebreakers and games have one important element in common—they often involve a lot of good, healthy touching. In chapter 6, I mention the vital importance of appropriate physical contact for healthy personal development. Being comfortable with appropriate touching will be helpful, if not essential, for successfully directing the games that I describe.

On the other hand, games and icebreakers have two very distinct uses. Icebreakers take up little time or space and can easily be tucked in before more substantial program offerings as hors d'oeuvres to whet the appetite for lively involvement. Games entail more time, space, and preparation; are a lot more active than icebreakers; and are most useful for parties, picnics, and other social celebrations. So here are four rowdy, crazy games whose sole purpose is maximizing the good times.

1. Musical Boys

People love this game as soon as they hear the title. But it gets better. The girls in the group each find a boy partner. The boys then get down on their hands and knees and form a circle with their head pointing toward the center. When the music starts, one boy is instructed to leave the circle, then the girls begin walking around the outside of the circle—just like in "Musical Chairs." When the music stops, the girls must each try to get a place on a boy's back—usually by grabbing him around the middle and hanging on for dear life. The girl who finds herself without a spot is permitted by the rules of the game to attempt to pull her rivals loose from their boys' backs; so a merry struggle often ensues as the liberated ladies fight for a firm grip on the gentlemen they have claimed. When the loser is established and sidelined, the music starts again, and another boy leaves the circle to set the stage for the next round, and so on. In the final contest, the two surviving girls circle around the one remaining boy, and if he trembles, who can blame him?

2. Newspaper Costumes

For this game, each team of four people receives a large stack of newspapers and a roll of masking tape. One member is elected to be the dummy (ah, make that "mannequin") on whom a tape and newspaper costume is built. The last time we played the game we ended up with, among other things, Big Bird, the Statue of Liberty, siamese twins, and several bizarrely buxom lady creatures. The activity finishes up with a fashion show—the costumed players parade through one at a time while another team member narrates. This game is a classic.

3. Bag Skits

Each team of four members receives a bag containing four assorted props—objects like a candle, a swimsuit, a hammer, and a roll of toilet paper. Each bag can contain different items, or all the teams can have the same set of props. The teams have twenty minutes to develop a skit that includes all four props, and then everybody comes back for the show.

4. Wink

"Wink" is a favorite from the book *More New Games* (New York: Doubleday, 1981). To begin the game, designate one person "it" and have everyone else find a partner. One member of each pair sits on the ground in a circle, facing the center. The other member of each pair kneels behind his or her partner, forming another circle outside the first one. "It" sits in the outer circle with a frisbee on the ground in front of him or her. "It" slyly looks about and winks at one of the "sitters," who instantly takes off on all fours toward the frisbee while the "kneeler" lunges forward and tries mightily to pounce, tackle, or otherwise prevent the scrambling "sitter" from touching the frisbee. At the moment of the wink, the whole group begins to chant, "one, two, three, four, five, six." Any "sitter" who gets to the frisbee by the count of six becomes "it." Any "sitter" who does not get to the frisbee in time becomes a "kneeler." Former "its" become new "kneelers." Does it sound complicated? It really isn't once you get going. And it's lots of fun.

A Pastoral Perspective

After thoroughly testing the four games in this chapter, our group heartily recommends them. Now I would like to make the case for games in more pastoral terms.

The Catholic church has a reputation of being unphysical, unhumorous, and therefore unhealthy. Young people, and adults too, are astonished when we invite them to let loose and enjoy life. Creating this kind of astonishment is one of the critical pastoral needs of our time. Without it, the young simply do not trust the rest of our good news.

Otie Doldt, a youth minister at Saint John's Parish in Chelmsford, Massachusetts, has grasped this principle and carried it to great heights. She has developed an annual affair called the "Dumb Games Olympics." She and her group find some of the games in the latest youth games literature, add a few they concoct themselves, and invite other youth groups to an afternoon of intense and absurd competition—complete with the olympic torch (an outdoor grill), kazoos playing the olympic theme song, homemade team T-shirts decorated with magic marker, and a painted rock trophy for the winning team. The afternoon ends with a picnic, a liturgy, and a time of songs and fellowship.

Another person with a strong appetite for absurd fun is Joe, a young man who is just graduating from our youth group. On his own, Joe organized a massive scavenger hunt for the teens of the town. About seventy-five high school students, in teams of five or six, showed up at his house at about 5:00 *p.m.* to get their lists of 154 items. The list contained things like Count Dracula's first name, a big magnet, a used tire, animal earmuffs, a duck, Maxwell's equations, a piece of moldy bread. There were only two rules: no buying and no stealing. At about 9:30 *p.m.*, cars full of loot began to fill up both sides of Joe's street. Anxious neighbors soon called the police about this sudden adolescent invasion. The police, with grim faces, rushed to the scene, but soon they were all smiles. They gladly gave their blessing to what they found. A team of judges, some of them teachers from the high school, peered into each car counting the findings. When at last a winning team was announced, the party at Joe's house began—and with no booze.

Yes, it's possible—just an outrageously good time that hurt no one and delighted everyone. An activity so lively that at first people assumed it had to be destructive turned out to be something positive and wonderful. The same thing happened at Pentecost. Peter stood up with the eleven and spoke with a loud voice, "'For these men are not drunk, as you suppose . . . This is what was spoken by the prophet Joel: "And in the last days it shall be, God declares, that I will pour out my Spirit upon all flesh, and your sons and daughters shall prophesy . . ."'" (Acts 2:15–17, RSV).

The people of God are learning again how to enjoy and celebrate life vigorously. The sons and daughters of the church have much to offer their peers who are stumbling about in search of life's true joys. Our young people will gladly pray, plan, and call their friends beyond the false joys of alcohol—and all the miseries that follow—if we will only dare to believe they can. Then we will find that the Kingdom of God can indeed be likened to a man who gave a party, a feast, a celebration.

3

You're Beautiful:
Affirming as a Fine Art

In order to do all the healthy experimenting and risking involved in growing up whole, young people need a very basic good feeling about themselves. But this is one psychological muscle they cannot build up by themselves. Somebody has to say, "Hey, you're great, do you know that? What? You don't? Well, you better face it! You are!" Helping others build up the muscle of self-esteem is called affirmation.

One young person, in a discussion about affirming people, talked about reaching the end of a long and difficult day and wondering why she was in such a good mood. She thought back and remembered that someone had given her a compliment way back in first-period English. That affirmation stayed with her and kept her spirits up all day long.

Few of us realize the significance of the gift we give when we point out the good in others. We all have this gift to give, but rarely do we give it. We are shy. We think that people already know their goodness. We're afraid to sound corny. We get stuck in envy. A thousand things stop us from building up one another's confidence, and we leave each other under-nourished. We all need a lot of affirmation, and the key to getting it is to give it, by "doing unto others what we would have them do unto us." The affirmation we initiate will come back around to us soon enough.

Thus, we must train our young people in the fine art of affirmation. The idea is to build youth communities in which personal qualities and strengths, as they emerge, are immediately recognized and generously encouraged. Here are some strategies:

1. The Back Stroke

The back stroke method of affirmation is light and easy. Group members each get big pieces of computer paper taped to their backs, and then they walk around the room and write on each other's papers the qualities that they see and like in them. The activity is fun and noisy, but it gets wonderfully quiet when people are given the signal to stop, sit down, and read their papers.

2. What's So Special?

For this exercise, give the following instructions one step at a time:
a. Pair off with a person whom you like and whose opinion you trust.
b. Take each other's hands and pray together that the Spirit of Truth will open your eyes so that you can truly see each other.
c. Now, for a full minute, take a good long look at your friend. Notice what is special to you, what means the most to you, about this person.
d. Take turns telling each other what good things you see in each other.

An aside: Five months after this exercise, one group member told me that during this exercise she had learned that she possesses the gift of noticing and lifting up people who are down. She has consciously been using this gift ever since.

3. Light Bags

On Friday night of a weekend retreat, tell everyone to hang up a brown lunch bag on a railing or wall and stick a name tag near the top identifying it as theirs. Then give everyone the "secret weapon," a little pad of paper that fits easily in a pocket. Tell everyone to look for Christ in everyone else and, when they see Christlike behavior, to sneakily note it on a piece of paper and stuff the note in the person's bag. The leaders should check late Saturday night to make sure that everyone's bag is comparably bulging. On Sunday afternoon, have everyone open their bag in small groups and share what they have learned about themselves. After the sharing, offer this suggestion: "Keep this little stack of truth and reread it whenever you start to feel you have nothing to offer."

4. You're Beautiful!

Have buttons made with the message "You're beautiful" printed on them in big red letters. In a group that has been together for a while, instruct the young people to go around and tell each other what's beautiful about them. When the young people have finished hearing how beautiful they are, give them their buttons. But before they pin them on, ask them, "Will you tell any person who reacts to your button something beautiful about him or her?" If they agree to back up their button with an affirming response, the initiation is complete, and they can pin on their button.

Urge the young people to give away their button to anyone who really likes it and promises to back it up. Then cheerfully replace any buttons that have been given away. Once one of our members gave his button to Boston's Cardinal Medeiros, who enjoyed the affirmation, then carefully listened to the conditions and solemnly promised to "back up his button."

A strong and healthy self-esteem cannot be built up through organized little exercises alone. Young people need to be immersed in affirmation for long periods of time. We all normally carry around in us information that would be quite affirming to one another, but we usually hold it back. So ultimately, the call to our young people is to go beyond exercises like the ones in this chapter and to affirm people spontaneously, as a regular part of their friendship style.

Often the big barrier to practicing affirmation is envy. We see a strength, and if we are still insecure and competitive, what we admire in others can secretly threaten us. But envy is simply affirmation that got lost on the way to its mark. So we can talk about misdirected affirmation and help one another to see that it's really an act of freedom and self-confidence to rejoice in the gifts of others. We need to challenge everyone to unlock our life-giving perceptions to one another and to get used to passing them on. Doing this surely comes within the context of Jesus' saying, "'And you will know the truth, and the truth will make you free'" (John 8:32, RSV). In fact, for all of us, these little chunks of truth are enormously freeing.

4

We Need a Dance:
Planning Great Dances

Sooner or later every youth minister hears the awful question "Can we have a dance?" And any youth minister who has answered "yes" says a silent "God help me!" at that same moment. For dances seem uniquely capable of calling forth the darkest side of the adolescent world: alcohol, drugs, violence, and sexual excess seem to be drawn almost magnetically to the exciting sound of Top 40 music. However, we youth ministers also sense that there is great potential for joy, community, and outreach in having a dance. So we give our consent and then wonder if it is possible to run a dance that is not an occasion of stress and anxiety, of a losing clash between the kingdoms of darkness and light. Is it possible to have a dance that will generate an atmosphere of fun and warmth, peace and goodness?

Our youth group used to hire a band, hire the police, advertise at the high school, and struggle through massive affairs with four to five hundred teens at a time. Soon we decided that it was not actually ministry, and even if it was, life was too short to carry such a load. So we stopped having dances for a few years. Then we found a different approach, and for four years or so, we've been having a wonderful time running enjoyable dances. One important condition of our approach is that the initiative for a dance must come from a youth group that has built some prior sense of community that it wishes to celebrate with a dance so that all the members see and feel that this is *their dance*.

Once a sense of community had been established in our group and the initiative for a dance had been expressed, we used the following steps as our formula for successful dances:

1. Some members of our youth community form a team, which includes an adult advisor, and plan the details—theme, music, refreshments, chaperones, decorations, cost, cleanup crew, and no police. They hire a teenage DJ, usually a youth group member, and part of the DJ's contract requires that she or he weed out any songs that proclaim non-Christian values.

2. The team then tells the youth community about its plans and says very firmly and clearly: "Invite whoever you want, but remember that you are responsible for the behavior of your guests. Explain to your guests that this dance is to honor Christ and his values in our community, so alcohol, drugs, violence, and sex have no place." (This kind of word-of-mouth promotion is all the advertising we do. The turnout now is 100 to 150 young people.)

3. A big group of members shows up earlier in the day to put up the decorations, which correspond to the dance's theme. (We usually order a pizza to keep ourselves going.)

4. One half-hour before the dance, the planning team does something called "praying down the Spirit." The team joins hands in a circle and invites Christ to come and be Lord of the dance. They ask aloud for every good thing they want this dance to bring about, and they pray against every bad thing that could spoil it. Now they are ready.

5. After people arrive, at around 8:00 *p.m.*, the DJ booms out over the mighty amplifiers a call to form a large circle. A member of the team then steps forward, takes the mike and says something like the following: "We dedicate this dance and everything we do tonight to Christ, and we ask him for the gift of a good time for all." And with that brief flourish of prayer, the lights fade and the music rises.

6. During the dance, the team and the chaperones both join in and keep a watchful eye on things. They make an effort to get to know new people and to dissolve the hard edges of cliques. Any difficult customers are ushered out, sometimes by a young person, sometimes by an adult. The territory is considered sacred, and protecting it is made much easier by the sense of God's presence and power, which has been called into everyone's consciousness.

7. The dance finishes at midnight; then the brooms and bags are brought out, and the cleanup is attacked en masse. The doors are usually locked by 1:00 *a.m.*, but not before the team gets together and sends up a prayer of thanksgiving.

The above steps have helped us plan dances that are occasions of joy for all of us. Only one dance in the last fifteen or so got crazy on us. We figured out afterward that the team was inexperienced and had forgotten to pray down the Spirit. It may not seem like you're doing much at the time, but the results of that little prayer have been pretty convincing to all of us.

The dancing itself often takes on a spontaneous quality that frees up even the most shy among us. People dance in groups as much as they do in pairs. During most dances, a new and broader level of trust and closeness builds up and breaks through. New friendships often begin, and the ongoing soap opera of the ever-changing loves of the teens proceeds full tilt. Yet, the young people are amazingly sensitive to any broken hearts and kindly lend hands of comfort to help one another through their storms.

It is clear to our youth community, and even to outsiders, that something special happens at our dances. We simply regard this specialness as the fulfillment of Christ's promise, "'. . . Ask, and you will receive, that your joy may be full'" (John 16:24, RSV).

5

The Subtle Oppressors:
Confronting Self-destructive Youth Trends

Once, after writing a column about youth ministry in our archdiocesan newspaper, a reader wrote and took me to task for ascribing problems with sex, alcohol, and other drugs to teenagers generally. She said, "I believe the majority of teens do not indulge in these activities; only a minority do. I think you are painting an unduly negative picture of teenagers, hardly an appropriate thing for a youth minister to do."

I welcomed her letter because it expressed a fierce love for young people. I dedicate this chapter to her and all others who share her faith in, and advocacy for, the generation now coming of age. Her confidence in young people is not misplaced. Extraordinary goodness does exist in young people, but this goodness is presently at risk.

I think everyone would agree that to truly love teens, or anybody else, a person has to really know them. So in this chapter, I take a good, hard look at statistics about some of the habits of this current generation of young people.

- 70 percent of U.S. high school students have tried marijuana, and 30 percent of seniors smoke it regularly.
- 30 percent of thirteen- to sixteen-year-olds and 60 percent of sixteen- to eighteen-year-olds have had sexual intercourse.
- 40 percent of today's twenty-year-old women were pregnant in their teens. Of these pregnant teenagers, 30 percent chose abortion, 30 percent chose adoption, and 40 percent kept their babies.

All of the above statistics can be found in a book compiled by John Roberto and published by the National Federation for Catholic Youth Ministry, *Foundations* (vol. 1 of *Readings in Youth Ministry* [Washington, DC, 1986], pp. 61, 66).

- 68 percent of U.S. teens consume alcohol at least once a month (U.S. Department of Health and Human Services, *National Trends in Drug Use and Related Factors Among American High School Students and Young Adults, 1975–1986,* 1987, p. 30).
- 65 to 70 percent of practicing Catholic teens in public schools see no moral objection to premarital sex (*Catholic Trends* 17 [6 September 1986]: 2).

What trends are we seeing in the youth subculture? First, it's important to realize that we are dealing with *majorities*. Second, indications are that these trends are all on the rise. And worse, the last statistic given suggests that Catholic young people are pretty much going along with what is developing in the teenage subculture as a whole.

How do we interpret and respond to the numbers? Here is a learn-by-mistake story from our youth group about interpreting and responding to trends and statistics:

At one of the many youth ministry workshops that come through our archdiocese, a speaker was asked about commissioning teenage peer leaders who are occasionally visible around town with a can of beer in their hands. He said, "You can't fight a trend that says 60 to 80 percent of teens drink socially. Chalk it up to 'boys will be boys,' and 'girls will be girls' and don't waste energy trying to change their social reality."

So I went back to our youth group, relieved at the trainer's down-to-earth advice, and said things that led our young people to believe that underage drinking is not that big of an issue. Five months later, a new ninth grade group member whose parents were away for the weekend was encouraged by some older members to host a beer party for virtually the whole youth group. The great majority attended and because such events do not stay secret for long, the youth community suddenly found itself in the midst of a crisis. We could not avoid the issue at our meetings. After much debate and searching of the Scriptures and our consciences, the group concluded that underage drinking, despite its prevalence, is destructive because it usually entails lying to parents; it always entails breaking the law; and it dishonors Christ by compromising the Christian witness of an individual or a group.

In this case, drinking emerged as the issue over which youth group members had to decide whether the challenge of following Christ was too socially inconvenient to accept. After this event, the youth group rebuilt itself with a new willingness to stand up against negative social influences. And the group's spiritual vitality was much improved.

Initially, the teens in our youth group were not equipped to take on the peer pressures of the youth culture, and the reason was simply that the adults weren't equipped either. The sheer size of the trends can discourage us from bringing up the very issues that our young people need to think about. Statistics about the teenage drinking trend prompted the trainer of youth ministers to discourage rather than encourage a strong Christian response to the problem. But after working for many years with teens in the midst of these real-life pressures, I have discovered that these statistics can equally well assist us to confront the problems they indicate. Here is what I found:

1. The numbers suggest a lot of experimentation rather than an established lifestyle. I have found that while experimenting, many teens are still trying to decide what's right for them, and they need to talk.
2. It's not just a teen problem. The adult culture in America is pretty well out of control in the same three areas: sex, alcohol, and drugs.
3. Catholic teens do not show up with a distinct identity apart from the general population of teens regarding these trends. Their thinking is being formed more by the culture than by the church. And that bit of news is a real ministry waker-upper.

To summarize, North American culture and its teen subculture are both in trouble regarding these trends, and our Catholic young people need adult Catholics who can help them name that trouble for what it is and think through values of their own in response.

I hope the woman who wrote to me because she cares about youth now joins me in seeing the needs indicated by the statistics. We're being called. And the call is for courage. Our young people see us finding the courage to oppose oppression of poor people at home and abroad, but they do not see us daring to oppose what oppresses them.

And the issue is oppression. Something alluring and destructive has hold of our young people. It deceives them about where to find joy, and it pressures them to conform. Young people need youth workers to help them see how their social patterns are diminishing their lives. But most of us, volunteer and professional alike, are silent. Why? Perhaps because our own Christian values about alcohol, drugs, and sex are not clear. I am convinced that we who live and work with parish teens must open up this tough, tough domain and start exploring it with our young people, telling our stories, listening carefully, and at times, speaking hard truths to soft thinking.

In this book, I usually offer a practical program of some sort to get at the problem at hand. This time I offer only what the above story offered—a parish youth community, with Christ in the center, in which the difference between Christian values and cultural values was carefully weighed and in which healthy choices and lifestyles found peer support. And I offer a scriptural passage that seems well-suited to the present situation: " . . . Where sin increased, grace abounded all the more" (Rom. 5:20, RSV). If this is really true, then we can expect a downpour of divine assistance when we create the space and opportunity for helping young people confront the trends in their culture that would prevent them from growing up whole, free, and yes, holy.

6

Go, Grab Someone:
Hugging and How It Helps

At a recent national youth ministry convention, a workshop on adolescent sexuality was especially popular. At first it was just the topic that drew attendance, but then word got around that Bob Bartlett was a dynamo of a man with a big heart for young people and lots of wise things to say. So I went to the workshop, and I learned that there are two kinds of families— touch families and no-touch families. Teens from no-touch families are much more prone to becoming sexually active because they are starved for physical contact. Mr. Bartlett challenged us to look at our own backgrounds and our own comfort with physical expressions of affection. Then he urged us to build youth groups that do a lot of hugging.

I get the same message every time I watch film footage of Mother Teresa. She is so physical. Her hands are always reaching out to stroke, hug, and hold, not just children, not just dying people, but everybody she comes in contact with. That's the word—*contact*. The word means more than "physical touch," and more than that is needed. But as Mother Teresa and Bob Bartlett tell us, a love that ignores our need to be touched does not fully satisfy.

We work at hugging in our youth community. And while hugging one another is freeing and fun, it still is work, and we still need a lot of practice, because most of us are still shy and resistant. We have to keep working at it, or we will find ourselves backing off again. Here are some ways we keep hugging alive in our youth group:

1. Every so often at a weekly youth meeting, I mention some research that established that humans need six hugs a day just to maintain and eight hugs a day to thrive. Then I ask people to hug at least three people so we all get our daily dosage.

2. Hellos and good-byes always entail hugs. If a young person is new and a bit unsure, I sometimes hold back, but most of the time I just explain that hugs are customary here and plant my hug gently but firmly.

3. If the community starts getting stingy about hugs, I initiate a discussion with the leadership group about whether to keep hugging as one of our priorities. People reveal their slight embarrassments but always renew, as leaders, their commitment to keep hugging alive and well among us.

4. If anyone arrives at a planning meeting burdened or withdrawn, I sometimes call for an impromptu "rite of peace" to get us together so the peace of Christ can flow freely among us. People laugh, chat, and enjoy themselves during this healing ritual, which almost always includes hugs. As a result, we all get nicely loosened up for our work together.

5. When someone needs prayer because they are about to give a talk or lead a meeting, or because they have some special need for comfort, we use a biblical style of prayer and gather round the person with a laying on of hands. The gentle touch, the gentle words, and the gentle faith that get expressed combine to be a great lifter of hearts.

6. Almost every time we pray as a group, we join hands in a large circle. This visible and tactile sign of unity is itself a powerful prayer.

7. Where would we be without games—imaginative and physical games that are designed not so much for competition but for the sheer playfulness and human contact that are basic youth ministry tools of the trade? (See chapter 2.)

8. Periodically we have everyone sit in a big back-rub circle. Before starting, we give some instruction about how to relieve the tension that builds up in the muscles that run from the shoulder to the neck. People on the receiving end are directed to provide constant feedback to their back rubbers, using some type of signal such as groans of pain or moans of ecstasy, or by saying "harder" or "softer" until the back rubber gets it right. Then after a bit, we change directions and ask everyone to rub the back of the person behind them. Lots of laughter and maybe even a bit of effective massage take place, but most of all, everyone has a good time being wholesomely physical together.

"People were bringing little children to [Jesus], for him to touch them. The disciples scolded them, but when Jesus saw this he was indignant. . . . He embraced them, laid his hands on them and gave them his blessing" (Mark 10:13,16, NJB). Touching and blessing cannot be easily separated. Jesus sometimes did heal at a distance, but whenever he could, he got his hands on the people who needed him. And so should we. Faith, when it just talks, may persuade; but when it also reaches out and touches, it does much more. Touch has the power to relax and the power to heal. So let's reach out with both hands for the hearts of our young.

7

Hi, Mom! Hi, Dad!
Re-bonding with Parents

Some developmental psychologists see parents as scratching posts for their young teenagers. The teenagers are like cats, sharpening their emerging powers of mind and will on the values and persons of their parents. At ages thirteen to fifteen, young people are often critical, self-righteous, and self-absorbed. They tend to define themselves by what they do not like. This age-span is often referred to as the stage of negativism.

That's the bad news, but there's good news just around the bend if parents can get through this adolescent equivalent of the "terrible twos." Around age sixteen (plus or minus a year), young people give birth to a wonderful capacity to go beyond self-preoccupation to discover others. They attain a capacity to fall in love—not just with a romantic partner, but with good friends, with significant adults, with life, and with God. This span from age sixteen to age twenty is often called the stage of romanticism.

In our youth group, I've watched the stage of romanticism occur with amazing regularity. Almost on schedule, at around age sixteen, two great concerns emerge: one is to go beyond the security of the group to the authenticity of individual relationships, the other is to go beyond the security of inherited beliefs to the firsthand discovery of Christ.

Most youth retreat movements in this country are based on this new readiness among young people to form deeper relationships and to meet the Lord. Young people naturally bestow on Christ their title of highest honor, *Friend,* because friendship is their term for reaching out and discovering the reality of other people.

In our youth community, we have found one other, perhaps unlikely, set of people with whom the teens can make friends—their parents. Teens making friends with their parents does not happen naturally and, in fact, amidst all the excitement of social and spiritual discovery, parents can easily be left out. But along with the need to define space independent from their parents, young people now have the capacity to break through to a new awareness of their parents as people. It is possible to assist the birth of this new relationship in a number of ways. For example, parents could come to a regular youth meeting as special guest participants once or twice a year; or parents of teens on retreat could stage a surprise welcome-home potluck, complete with decorations, singing, and their young people's favorite dishes. But the best thing our group does, and we do it over and over again, is give parents a special opportunity to relate to and support their teens in their spiritual search. The following is a condensed version of the letter we use to explain this opportunity to parents:

Dear Parents,

Your son or daughter has signed up for the upcoming youth retreat. I am writing to ask you to participate in the retreat in a special way.

Doing *palanca* is a tradition of the Cursillo movement, and it has become a highly valued tradition for our retreats as well. *Palanca* is the Spanish word for "winch" or "crank." It means strategically applying a small effort in order to produce a great lifting power. "Doing *palanca*," then, is a special way of praying that is used to assist people making a major spiritual effort. It is prayer with an action component.

The first part of doing *palanca* is to pray for your son or daughter and then to *do* something to back up your prayer. For instance, along with your prayer intentions you may choose to fast by skipping a meal; by not eating snacks between meals; or by avoiding cigarettes, sweets, or television. Or you may choose to do a special act of generosity, such as washing the dishes all weekend, attending an extra Mass as a prayer for your young person, being patient with that certain person who gets to you, or saying a rosary. The action you select adds substance to your praying and multiplies its effect.

The second part of doing *palanca* is to write a letter to your son or daughter before the retreat and to secretly slip it to us for delivery during the retreat. The letter should reveal your prayer for them, describe the extra thing you are doing, and express your support and hopes for their retreat experience. The letter should have the character of a love letter, affirming what is beautiful in your son or daughter. The letters will be given to the young people at a key moment in the retreat. I encourage you to invest a lot of time and thought into this opportunity. It can do great things for your relationship with your son or daughter.

I hope you will enjoy doing *palanca*.

Yours in Christ,
[Youth Leader]

I've watched teens weep as they read these letters from home. And I'll never forget one young person saying, "He would do that for me?" Sometimes at the end of a retreat, a young person will shyly admit, "The letter I got from my mom was what best conveyed the Lord's love to me."

One caution: Make sure that all the young people have a letter from a parent or a guardian. If someone does not, make a substitute provision for that person, by writing a letter yourself or by discreetly giving special care and attention to that person at the time that the letters are opened.

The purpose of these and all our efforts to build a bridge of understanding between the generations draws us into the very last verse of the Hebrew Scriptures: "'And [Elijah] will turn the hearts of fathers to their children and the hearts of children to their fathers, lest I come and smite the land with a curse'" (Mal. 4:6, RSV).

And it is a curse when young adults come of age alienated from their parents. But we can help bring about a great blessing—young adults who have gained not only a respect for, but a friendship with, their parents.

8

Stand Up to the Boss:
Coaching the Part-time Worker

North American teenagers have gone to work. The *Boston Globe* reports that the number of work permits issued by schools more than doubled in the last two years (Patricia Wen, "Learn or Earn," 11 January 1988). *Group* magazine, quoting a survey by the University of Michigan Institute for Social Research, reports that 80 percent of high school seniors across the country hold part-time jobs ("News, Trends, and Tips," 13 [October 1987]: 12). I have noticed in my work with teens that once they are sophomores, it is rare to find a young person without a job.

The employment surge among young people is a recent phenomenon, and for a while, I saw it as a good thing. True, most jobs for youth are at the bottom of the economic ladder, but the experience of producing in the "real world" must surely be good for them.

I now see the employment of youth as a mixed blessing at best. The following story will illustrate:

As the school year began, I watched a young person who liked her job be asked (by a boss she also liked) to work more and more hours, until she was working about eighteen hours a week. Her grades, her other activities, her friendships, and her sense of well-being all suffered. She was a helpful and trusting person, and it just never occurred to her that her kindly employer, who needed all these hours from her, was using her, with little consideration of her needs. She finally caught on, stood up to his pressure, and insisted on a schedule that was right for her.

This young woman experienced oppression. The *Boston Globe* article "Learn or Earn" exposes some of the difficulty of teenage jobs:

> Some employers in dire need of workers admit that teen-agers are pushed to work long hours and that they wait until hearing a complaint from a student before cutting back hours.
>
> "Being brutally honest, you get so desperate for help you work these kids so hard," said one manager of a fast-food restaurant, who asked to remain anonymous. "You burn these kids out."

The employer quoted is talking about job burnout. My concern is overall personal burnout. Even before the present employment surge, it was often noted among youth ministers that teens, compared to all other age-groups, have by far the busiest schedules. Now that stress is being tightened one notch higher. As an age-group, teenagers are certainly strong and resilient, but there are trouble signs showing in the familiar symptoms of alcohol consumption, violence, pregnancy, drug abuse, depression, and suicide. As we puzzle about the forces at work in teenagers' lives, I propose that one big cause of the pain and confusion is their crushing daily schedules now that part-time work has become so pervasive.

Exploitation of young workers, whether intentional or not, can easily happen. Young people have been trained at home, at school, and at church to respect and obey the adults in their life. I quite often find teens working more hours than is good for them, and they often find themselves scheduled at times they have said they could not work. Their bosses schedule them anyway and they take it, for two reasons: they do not want to defy their elders, and they do not want to jeopardize their paycheck.

Educators have a vested interest in the problem of teens working too many hours. Research correlating jobs and grades found that students who worked up to twenty hours a week improved their grades, while students who worked more than twenty hours a week fell behind in their studies (Wen, "Learn or Earn"). The University of Michigan Institute for Social Research reports that over half of the high school seniors who work say their job interferes with their education ("News, Trends, and Tips," p. 12).

Youth ministers also have a vested interest in the problem. Youth programs all over the Archdiocese of Boston are seeing a sharp decline in attendance both at special events and at Mass. Apparently, many teens are working rather than participating in church activities.

Parents too have a vested interest in the problem. Quality time for the family to be together and to do things together is now quite scarce. For all practical purposes, childhood is ending several years before graduation, and a significant chunk of growing-up time has been lost.

But none of our adult groups, as much as we do care, has as great a vested interest in solving this problem as do the teens themselves.

While adults cannot solve the problem for the young people, they can offer their help—help similar to the kind the church provides for oppressed people in various places all over the world, help primarily aimed at building the young people's confidence in their own value as persons and in their ability to solve their own problems.

In chapter 20 of this book's companion volume, *Create Community with Christ,* I present an approach called the "values workshop" that can be used to help the young people deal with troubles that stem from out-of-control schedules. The strategy is to think with them about the connection between their schedule-making decisions and their quality of life.

The rest of the material in this chapter shows how we applied the steps from the values workshop to the problem of schedule balancing. You can use this material to stimulate your young people to think through their own values in relation to their daily schedules.

1. The Values Problem

We raised the following questions in our group discussion on schedule balancing:

- How do you know when your schedule is unbalanced and unhealthy?
- What are the ingredients of a balanced schedule?
- What attitudes should young people take toward the pressures and demands of employers?

2. Possible Alternatives and Consequences

These questions helped us focus on the consequences of our busy schedules:
- What ingredients do teens typically neglect when their schedules get tight?
- What are the consequences of leaving out these ingredients?

3. The Advice of the Scriptures and the Church

Next, we turned to the Scriptures and the church for advice on dealing with our schedule-related problems:

"Come to me, all you who labor and are overburdened. . . ." (Matt. 11:28, NJB)

" . . . You cannot be the slave both of God and of money." (Matt. 6:24, NJB)

"So do not worry; do not say, 'What are we to eat? What are we to drink? What are we to wear?' . . . Your heavenly Father knows [what you need]. Set your hearts on his kingdom first. . . ." (Matt. 6:31–34, NJB)

" . . . Love your neighbour as yourself." (Matt. 22:39, NJB)

The most helpful scriptural passages seem to come from Matthew. Maybe because Matthew was a former tax collector, he had the most experience with money issues.

The Catholic church's advice to working people worldwide has been given in a number of Vatican documents over the past fifty years. The message is simple: workers must stand up for their rights, and employers must be challenged by laws, unions, and individuals whenever they take advantage of their workers.

4. The Search for Values

After thoroughly discussing the issues related to schedule balancing, the following values emerged:
- Treat your employer as a respected equal, not as an elder, and bargain for a contract or work agreement that gives equal respect to your priorities and to his or hers.
- Do not allow your employer to add conditions later on—such as overscheduling or underpaying—that are contrary to the initial agreement.
- The elements worth including in a healthy schedule are study time, relaxation time, family time, social time, work time, and church time.
- An inner sense of well-being is the yardstick you can use as an indicator of whether your schedule meets all your needs.

Once the young people have arrived at some values about balance in their daily schedule, they can go to work on re-shaping the pattern and pace of their life.

An additional condition: In helping individuals solve their schedule-related problems, the four-step approach outlined in this chapter can be useful. However, one additional condition is needed: the young people must want to seek the best possible Christian solution. This condition should be established before taking step one. As the young people work their way through the rest of the steps, two temptations will normally surface. One temptation is to give inordinate value to the things their money can buy. Clothes, cars, and even tuition savings are not worth the academic, spiritual, and personal decline that results from overwork. (Adults may also be caught in this temptation.) The other temptation teens face is to be fearful about valuing and asserting their own needs. Young people will actually gain rather than lose respect in the eyes of most employers if they possess the confidence to stand up for what is right for themselves. That confidence as well as a firm standard of inner peace, which they need to create for themselves, will stand them in good stead all through their adult life.

Does the value of an inner sense of well-being as it applies to the part-time jobs teens take have any scriptural support? Well, Jesus not only offers peace, "'. . . My peace I give to you . . . let not your hearts be troubled,'" he also asks it of his disciples: "'Peace be with you'" (John 14:27; 20:19, RSV). If we consider ourselves disciples, we can take these words as instructions to receive and maintain a wonderful peace. Anytime we lose that peace, we can be sure things are not as they should be. We need to search for the causes of our loss of peace and make some changes. Sometimes an inner change of attitude will do the trick, but more often radical pruning of the schedule will be necessary if our young people's lives are to be happy and productive.

9

What's Come Over You?
Dealing with the Occult

My nine-year-old son can walk into our local toy store and buy a Ouija board. No one will consider him underage and no surgeon general's warning appears on the box. But it should. I will illustrate.

Mike, at age fifteen, had some fun with a Ouija board one weekend with a small group of friends. The "voice" they contacted was fascinating, and beyond that, nothing very scary happened. But that night, Mike had a "weird feeling," and he could not get to sleep. Every day after that when he found himself alone at home, he felt "spooky."

Mike was a stable, sociable young person. He played football and took his religion seriously, but this thing was bigger than Mike could handle. After several weeks of feeling as if he was "walking around under a shadow," Mike told his dad and his uncle. They told Mike to just hang on, to not be afraid, and this thing would pass. Their firm assurance gave Mike confidence, and gradually the weird feelings went away. I heard about all this from Mike a few months later, because

Mike was now concerned about some friends who were getting even deeper into the occult.

Most people think of Ouija boards, palm readers, séances, and other such things as fascinating and harmless parlor games. But they can be far from harmless, and their use among young people is widespread. For some, the voices and the uncanny knowledge they encounter are oddities they soon forget, while for other more vulnerable young people, contact with the "spirit world" exerts an attraction and fills a void. The parlor games can be the first steps into occult involvement, cultic ritual, and seriously destructive behavior.

When teens come to us in distress as a result of dabblings in the occult, we need two resources to help them: an informed perspective about what's really going on, and a remedy to relieve the distress. The following anecdote describes both of these resources and demonstrates how they can work in our ministries to teens.

Jessica came to me in great fright. She had visited a psychic. The man had done a reading and concluded that Jessica had sustained several head injuries with mild concussions. Jessica was amazed and impressed—it was true. "And you will die of head injuries in an auto accident within a year." That's strong stuff for a sixteen-year-old.

"The psychic was right about my head injuries; he must be right about my death," Jessica reasoned. She desperately pleaded with me, "Is there anything I can do?"

Here's what I told her:

Jessica, you've just taken in a dose of fear. And that fear itself proves this message is not from God. Do you know someone counted 365 separate passages in the Bible that say, "Do not be afraid"? That's one for every day in the year. Did you know John's first letter says, "' . . . Perfect love drives out fear . . .'" (1 John 4:18, NJB)? And in that same chapter John says, "'My dear friends, not every spirit is to be trusted, but test the spirits to see whether they are from God . . .'" (1 John 4:1, NJB).

The message of that psychic did not come from the Spirit of God but from the other kind of spirit, and fear is one of the evil spirits' specialties. Fear and also lies. Yes, there is such a being as Satan and also evil spirits. Jesus calls Satan "'the father of lies'" (John 8:44, NJB). The strategy of the Kingdom of Evil is to pass off distortions of the truth that will knock down our faith, our hope, and our love. That's what has happened to you. By way of the psychic, the spirit of evil has twisted some accurate information so as to intimidate you.

All through the Gospels we see Jesus commanding evil spirits who have gotten access to people's minds to release them, and in Mark's Gospel, Jesus tells us that even we can do the same. "'These are the signs that will be associated with believers: in my name they will cast out devils . . .'" (Mark 16:17, NJB). You aren't possessed by any means, but the spirit of fear does have its hooks into you. Here's what I recommend: let's put Jesus' words into practice. First, pray with me and renounce your belief in that evil message. Then put your trust and life back in the hands of God, and order the fear to leave your mind and heart.

Jessica did what I recommended, and a very relieved young woman walked out of my office. She outlasted that false prophesy and the last I heard of her, she was married and had a family.

As modern, educated North Americans, we have a dilemma. We tend not to believe in Satan or evil spirits, yet 25 percent of all Jesus' healings dealt with deranged people whose demons he had cast out. And our Catholic tradition supports belief in Satan and in the demonic. We are left with an uncomfortable choice between our culture and our church. I urge you to entertain the traditional belief. I propose to you, in fact, that the traditional position empowers us to minister effectively to the rising tide of problems associated with the occult and that the pseudosophistication of the culture's disbelief leaves those problems unresolved.

Effective ministry in this area is greatly needed. *Group* magazine did a feature article entitled "Kids Seduced by Satan," by Rick Chromey (15 September 1989). Chromey compares fascination with Satan and the occult to alcohol addiction—easy to fall into, tough to break out of. He details the progressive stages of involvement in the occult. Fascination with the demonic often begins with occult parlor games. Then, pushed along by curiosity or desire for power or peer pressure, a vulnerable young person can be drawn into witchcraft and Satanism. And many observers agree that out-and-out Satan worship is a growing problem in our country.

What can we do by way of prevention in our youth groups and CCD classes? Certainly Satanism is not a topic to dwell on because the subject itself exerts a perverse fascination that can actually defeat the purpose of prevention. But, at the same time, the subject cannot be set aside. The following ten points have proven to be helpful as a base of information young people need and can use to respond wisely to the allurements of the occult:

1. The appetite for direct experience with hidden supernatural realities exists in all of us, and it can only be fully and positively satisfied in our encounters with God.

2. Satan's Kingdom of Evil does exist. It attacks those most vulnerable to its attraction, and its purpose is to ruin people's lives by turning them from God and tempting them to behavior that is destructive to themselves or others.

3. Because adolescence is naturally a time of flux and experimentation, young people are more readily affected by the attractions of the occult and the powers of evil.

4. Vulnerability to negative spirituality can be greatly increased by abuse in any of its many forms or by any other condition that prevents healthy personal development and growth.

5. Our society is presently being inundated with a tremendous variety of evil trends, such as violence, abortion, suicide, drug and alcohol abuse, promiscuity, indifference to poor people, child abuse, homelessness, racism, and so on. Evil trends like these can make anyone, and young people especially, more vulnerable to the occult and the powers of evil. Young people and adults whose lives are kept stable through faith and prayer are needed to be a healing and occult-proofing influence for those who have been hurt by the above realities.

6. Dabblings in the occult are prompted not only by the powers of evil but also by peer pressure and one's own selfish desires. For catechetical purposes, the Bible and traditional terms for those other two sources of temptation are the *world* and the *flesh*.

7. There is no need to fear evil powers because they can only cause harm to those who choose to be involved with them.

8. Anyone who has gotten stuck in any aspect of evil can be freed by talking and praying with someone of strong faith, by identifying the distresses that created the vulnerability, and by celebrating the sacrament of reconciliation. (See chapter 20.)

9. One of the specialties of the Blessed Mother is defeating the power of Satan. That's why she is so often depicted with a foot crushing the head of a serpent. The rosary is an extremely potent weapon to use on behalf of yourself or anyone else in trouble with some form of evil.

10. Our effectiveness in helping others who have become confused by evil depends on our speed in dealing with, and getting free from, anything in our own life that robs us of peace.

In our group, discussions that raise the above points are initiated several times a year. I say discussions because even though some of these basic ideas can be conveyed in the form of a talk, most of them are best dealt with in the context of a free-flowing dialog in which the young people report their experiences and ask their questions. With a dialog, we can learn more about the young people, even as they are learning a lot more about their faith and its resources for their life.

I have one final suggestion: sessions dealing with the occult should be preceded and protected by extra helpings of prayer, not only by the teen and adult leaders, but also by other parish people who are willing to intercede for the teens of their community. Empowered in this way, we will share the experience of the first disciples who "returned with joy and said, 'Lord, even the demons submit to us in your name'" (Luke 10:17, NIV).

10

The Importance of Getting Caught: Confronting Crime in Youth Groups

Occasionally parents have expressed to me a feeling of reassurance just knowing that their sons or daughters are involved with other young people from church. While there is some basis for that secure feeling, I always hasten to advise those parents not to assume too much.

In Matt. 9:13, Jesus says, "'. . . For I came not to call the righteous, but sinners'" (RSV). So I ask parents to realize that the young people in the youth group are not saints yet. I also ask them to not be too surprised when the youth group runs into crises and to understand that sometimes the group must invest significant amounts of time and energy in dealing with the sins of its members.

Confronting crime when it happens is an important agenda of any youth group, and the resolution of crises greatly benefits all members. In this chapter, I will present several true stories of serious violations that occurred in our youth group. These crises challenged us all to find a response that was wise and good.

Crises arise in our youth group about once every two years, and they represent a moment of great personal upheaval for the wrongdoers as well as for the group. In selecting which stories to tell, I have contacted a number of people who have long since gone into adulthood, and I want to offer special thanks to those who have generously allowed me to tell their stories so that others might benefit from their mistakes. Names have been changed but the facts have not.

Crime Story 1

The first crime occurred early in my ministry at Saint Agnes Parish, and it happened at the beach. A group of sophomores from our youth group developed an outdoor event for a large group of their school friends. Eighty teens in two buses rode off to a beautiful deserted beach one afternoon in the early spring. We picnicked, played volleyball and Frisbee, roamed the dunes, and capped the day with an open-air Mass.

While waiting for the return of our buses, a number of young people—too large a number—crammed into a small snack shop built onto the owner's house, and things got out of hand. The shop owner's family could not possibly serve a crowd that big, and the young people began to get loud and rowdy. Food was just taken off the racks, a table was broken, and several young people wandered into the owner's house and stole some jewelry.

Finally the buses came, and we all rode home, stunned to know that some of our number had seriously violated not only those shop owners but also the good name of the whole group. The wrongdoers would not step forward, and the youth group members leading the event were unwilling to turn in their names.

Instead, at an emergency meeting the following night, the youth group members decided to run a spaghetti dinner to raise a hundred dollars or so, which was the estimated loss to the victims of the crime. The parish heard the whole story, and the turnout was excellent. We invited as guests of honor the family members we had hurt, and they gladly came. They accepted the check, which was handed over with great ceremony, and responded with many expressions of gratitude for the goodness of most teens, especially those who were willing to make right what a few of their friends had done. The night was one of great joy.

The moral of this story is, *turning a bad situation into something good is often possible.*

Crime Story 2

This second crime story also involved a victim who was not part of the youth group. And again, several committed members of the youth group were present as witnesses. But this time, even though the perpetrator was an active youth group member, the deed was done apart from any youth group event. This factor initially served to dilute a sense of collective responsibility, even though everyone present was active in the youth group.

Here's what happened: A seventeen-year-old used a bat to smash the front of a pickup truck that was often parked in a place where the young people deemed it to be obstructing traffic. One troubled witness told me about what happened but would only tell me who the other onlookers were, not who the vandal was. Only after a series of sessions did the friends of the wrongdoer move from the street code (that is, peer loyalty as the basic moral principle) to a higher code (that is, care about everyone involved whether you know them or not, and whether or not the culprit thinks it's an expression of care). The vandal was finally identified, the truck owner was contacted, and several hundred dollars of restitution was made, without any involvement of parents or police.

The moral of this story for the witnesses is, *we are responsible for every bit of injustice we have the power to undo.* The moral for the vandal is, *when a community—especially a praying community—is involved, the truth will come out, and a way can be found to make things right.*

That crime was hard and slow to resolve, but my point is that great learning is possible for everyone who is touched in any way by a crime. And for the sake of this learning, the time and trouble it takes to resolve things fully is time and trouble well-spent. Violations of the law will probably occur as a youth group attracts more and more members. And when a crime occurs, you can expect the youth group to respond with a whole range of feelings—anger, sadness, disillusionment with their fellow Christians, and so on. To help the young people express and deal with whatever they feel, adult leaders should be open about their own feelings and should look for a way to add a faith note. For example: "Distressing as this crisis is, valuable lessons are waiting here for everyone." We can and should approach these crime crises as incomparable teachable moments, even allowing ourselves a quiet smile of inner anticipation of the good we can expect to reap.

Crime Story 3

The third story involves a theft, and this time the youth group itself was the victim. Someone stole $150, which I had carelessly left on my desk after taking retreat deposits at a youth meeting. I announced the theft the following week at our meeting, and the group prayed for the culprit and for recovery of the money.

The young man who did it needed money for Christmas shopping. He was an active youth group member and prayed for the thief right along with the rest of us. After a week or so, we found a note in our prayer bottle: "Please pray for me. I took the money and I don't know what to do." Pray we did, and pretty soon the guilty party, who happened to have a particularly expressive face, began to betray himself with a pained and haunted look. I took a chance. Privately and gently, I confronted him. He was only too relieved to spill the whole story, go to confession, and repay the money over a period of months.

The young man's identity was kept confidential when the good news of the thief's repentance and restitution was announced. The group received the news with great joy, in which he shared.

The moral of this story is, *it is important for group members who steal from the youth community to get caught.* Compassionate firmness is a necessary attitude for the whole youth community to have, for two reasons. First, such firmness heads off the mistaken idea that Christlike love is weak and the youth program an easy target for abuse. Second, the wrongdoers, once apprehended, have a chance to confess and repair what would otherwise remain inside them as festering guilt.

Parting Thoughts

My advice to youth ministers regarding crime within the youth group is threefold:
1. Do not be surprised when you sometimes find yourself in a role somewhere between detective and social worker—this role goes with the youth ministry territory.
2. Be prepared to challenge any values that surface in the youth group's reactions to wrongdoing that reflect the vengefulness or indifference of the culture. These are great teachable moments.
3. Prayer is the key to finding out "whodunit." And once you know, prayer is also the key to finding a wise response.

Jesus did not flinch from challenging the crowd to examine their own values when they were accusing the woman caught in adultery: ". . . 'Let the one among you who is guiltless be the first to throw a stone at her'" (John 8:7, NJB). But neither did he flinch from naming as sin what the young woman had done: ". . . 'Go away, and from this moment sin no more'" (John 8:11, NJB).

The fact that an action is illegal as well as morally wrong simply strengthens the moral authority we can bring to bear on it. In our overly psychological generation, which looks too quickly for excusing causes, a clear moral tone is much needed. Only then can clear decisions of repentance and restitution be made; and what's even more valuable, moral clarity can be added to the decision-making tools of the young persons as they move into more responsible positions in both our church and our society.

11

Do Not Hide That Pain: Helping Young People Deal with Loss

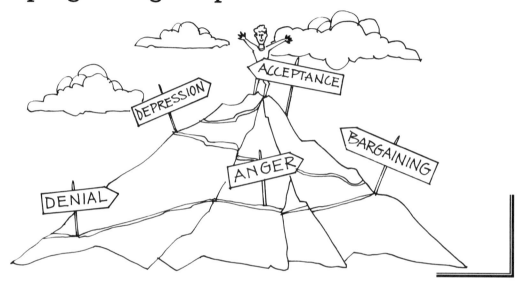

At the 1989 New England Consultants Conference in Hartford, one speaker told us about a survey of young people's greatest fears and worries. The death or divorce of parents was among the items most often mentioned. Another speaker told us that from now on, we could expect over half the teens in our youth groups to be from homes lacking one of their original parents. When I put these two facts together, it dawned on me that for a large percentage of our young people, *some of their worst fears are coming true.* This means that an awful lot of our youth must be carrying around a terrible load of loss and heartbreak.

As I drove home, mulling over that depressing thought, the work of Elisabeth Kübler-Ross came to mind. She is the respected doctor who is teaching our generation that the final months and days for the terminally ill can be a time of much growth, and even of peace, if honest feelings are allowed to surface. Kübler-Ross has made a less well known, but equally significant, contribution to people who have suffered profound loss. Her contribution is a powerful tool called "grief-work." Paralleling the five psychological stages of dying, the tool maps out five distinct stages in the experience of grieving and clarifies what does and does not help a grieving person move from the pain of serious loss to recovery. (See *On Death and Dying* [New York: Macmillan, 1969], pp. 148–159.)

By the time I reached home, I had decided to find a way to put the grief-work tool into the hands of the young people in our parish. In this chapter, I will report what took place.

First, I will tell the story of a young woman named Annette who, with the help of the Kübler-Ross stages, made the painful journey from a devastating loss to a real peace.

Then, I will present a grief-work training session designed to help young people work through current unprocessed losses and prepare them to work with losses yet to come. Our youth leaders developed the training session to counteract a tendency we all have to bury the pain of loss and try to hide it rather than to suffer it, deal with it, and bring it out into the light for healing.

Annette's Story

Because of her unusual faith and personal courage, Annette's journey through grief was a powerful testimony that opened up our youth group's attitudes toward loss and grief. Annette made Kübler-Ross's five-stage map of grief-work concrete and convincing.

Late in her sophomore year, Annette fell in love with a young man named Al. Both of them had strong personalities, and the relationship was stormy. The love between them was intense, but Al's drinking was a constant intruder in their relationship. Though still very much in love with Al, Annette broke off the relationship. A few months later, Al was killed in an alcohol-related car accident.

The impact of this news sent Annette reeling. She had been an enthusiastic student council member and a baton squad captain, but now she had no desire to be involved in any extracurricular activities. She talked endlessly about Al: "Why had he died? Couldn't God have done something? What if I hadn't broken up with him—would he still be alive?" Even Annette's best friends grew tired of her tragic story. She tried hanging out with Al's old friends, but they had a strange way of ritually denying Al's death by doing the same things they had always done when Al was alive and with them. Al's friends did not want to admit that things had changed.

Annette tried to go back to routine living, but the sadness was so deep that everything seemed meaningless. She wondered if she would ever be able to simply live and be happy again. She could no longer stand imposing her sadness on others, but at the same time, she could not stand masking it.

Every month or so, Annette and I would talk. She began to realize that she harbored bitter feelings toward God. She even stayed away from Mass a few times in protest to a God who would not spare a searching young man's life. However, Mass was often her best means for struggling with what was happening to her, a way of asking Christ what he was trying to teach her, a time for searching for answers. Gradually Annette realized that she needed to let go of Al and place him fully into the hands of God. Letting Al go was very hard. For a while Annette tutored disabled children as an outlet for her anguished love, and little by little, she did let go.

When spring came, Annette met someone new, David, and found—to her astonishment—that an outcome of her struggle and resolve was an unexpected freedom and capacity to love again. This gift grew from her unselfish love for Al in letting him go. During the summer, with David's patient help, Annette was finally able to say the prayer that surrendered Al to God. Death was not an end but a profound change. Annette felt that now she could live again, and so could Al.

My relationship with Annette had simply involved listening to her, praying with her, and doing one other thing. I kept before her, as a lifeline of hope, Kübler-Ross's map of grieving and its wonderful destination—acceptance and peace. Providing the map was not a large contribution from me; the larger ingredients were the faith and courage of that young woman. But that map rang true to her experience and offered stepping-stones on the path to healing.

My experience with Annette convinced me even more that other young people, carrying similar kinds of devastating loss, need the hope and wisdom of Kübler-Ross's map of grief stages. Thus, the idea for a grief-work training session was born.

Grief-Work Training Session

Originally the training session was to focus on the most extreme kinds of loss, such as death and divorce. However, on the advice of our youth priest, we widened the scope to include all kinds of losses. This broad focus allowed every person to identify closely with the training, even those who

had not yet been touched by heavy losses. The session had five distinct parts:
1. an introduction
2. an initial partner dialog
3. a presentation of the stages of grief-work
4. a witness (Annette's story)
5. a response dialog

Introduction

I introduced the topic to the group by saying something like this:

> Grieving is the emotional and spiritual work you must do to resolve the pain of losing someone or something you love very much. We all have a tendency to avoid the pain of loss by denying or ignoring the loss that caused it or by pretending the pain isn't there. People can go on like that, even for years, but the pain doesn't actually go away. The pain gets buried, and along with the pain, a lot of other feelings are buried that otherwise would be felt and expressed. As a result, an individual becomes less alive, less of a person, and, underneath, the aching just goes on and on. This session will teach you how to unbury those feelings and move through sadness to a point of again feeling very much alive and peaceful about who or what you lost.

Initial Partner Dialog

Then I asked point-blank: "Is it true that sooner or later we're all going to face losses that hurt us terribly?" The "yes" came back quite readily. "Then this session tonight is very important preparation for all of us! Now I would like you to pair off with someone whom you feel that you can talk with openly." After everyone paired up, I introduced the partners' dialog:

> Often when people think of going through serious grief, they mean mourning over the death of a loved one. But there are other kinds of difficult loss. With your partner, name some other kinds of losses people your age might sometimes go through.

The pairs then shared with the group the losses they had identified.

I used the list of possible losses on page 64 to supplement the group's list. Between what the group came up with and what I could add, most of the losses people were likely to be carrying got named. I wrote them on a chalkboard.

- Parents separate or get divorced.
- The one you love breaks up with you.
- You move.
- A longtime friendship ends.
- A parent loses his or her job.
- You or someone close to you terminates a pregnancy.
- You or someone close to you leaves for college.
- You or someone you love experiences financial disaster.
- You are unjustly accused of something.
- Your pet dies.
- Your house burns down.
- An adult you respect violates your trust.
- You or someone close to you sustains a disabling injury.
- A longtime plan is ruined.
- You get fired from your job.
- Your favorite possession is stolen or destroyed.
- Your favorite team loses an important game.
- You fail at an attempt to achieve an important goal.

After the list had been generated, I said something like the following:

> Okay, how many of you see something on this list that you have been through? Am I right that all these losses hurt enough so that recovery is difficult? That's the point of this session, to help you learn how to recover completely. Because loss is a basic part of life—we all will face it if we haven't already.

The Stages

Then, with broad-tipped markers, I wrote the titles of the five stages of grief-work on the panels of connected paper (computer paper works well) so that they could be displayed by revealing one stage at a time. I briefly introduced Dr. Kübler-Ross as the author of the five stages of grief-work, and then I held up the piece of paper on which the title of stage one was written. One by one, I described the stages feelingly (to help the young people catch the mood of each stage) as follows:

1. Denial

Denial is an initial reaction of refusal to believe the loss has actually occurred. For instance: "You're joking, aren't you?" or "This can't be happening." And it's not just words—it's also a decision to act for a while as if nothing has happened. We attempt to push the reality away by reasserting ordinary reality. To let in the reality of the loss would be to let in more pain and sadness than we think we can bear, so the door is slammed shut. If that attitude doesn't gradually give way, no grief-work can occur and we will have to live a life of superficiality, pretense, stress, and avoidance of everything that might touch deep feelings.

2. Anger

As the awful reality of the loss begins to sink in, the first feeling that comes is anger. Maybe we direct it at the person we've lost, maybe at ourselves, maybe at anybody handy, maybe at those seen as responsible for the loss, or maybe at God. We hate what has happened. We hate the pain of someone or something we love being torn away from us, and we want to blame someone. We rage, "Why did you let this happen?" Actually, feeling this anger is a positive sign, and letting this rage out is a necessary step toward healing. In fact, it's often the people who do not let out their anger who end up freezing the anger inside themselves, causing a permanent chilling of their capacity to feel at all. Rage can be expressed without being destructive, especially if it's directed against God. Job, Jeremiah, and Elijah all had moments of anger like that. God can handle rage. So can a lot of people who have experienced that rage and now understand it.

3. Bargaining

When anger is spent, an awareness of helplessness takes over, "I can't control what is happening, but maybe God can. Nothing is beyond God's control." We begin to make big promises to God. For instance: "I'll go to Mass every day" or "I'll change my ways" or "I'll give vast sums to charity." Bargaining is a last effort to regain control of events that are beyond our control by doing something so good it will obligate God to change things back to the way they were before.

Denial, anger, and bargaining are all ways of fighting the loss—denial by rejecting it, anger by lashing out at it, bargaining by trying to regain what was lost. With each reaction, we are moving ahead—letting in and facing more and more of the reality of the loss.

4. Depression

Now finally we face the reality of our loss. We have no defenses left, and the full meaning of the loss hits home.

The full realization of what we had, and won't have anymore, sinks in. The extent of our love for what we had is exposed by the extent of our pain from its loss. The depression we now feel is often as physical as it is emotional. We are too miserable to eat or sleep or study or see anyone. All we can do is hurt. The pain is terrible and life itself feels terrible. We may feel at this point what Jesus expressed on the cross, "'My God, my God, why have you forsaken me?'" (Matt. 27:46, NJB). At this point, most of all, we need someone to help us let all that feeling out.

5. Acceptance

By expressing just how we feel, we make room for the realization that others who love us, especially God, are not standing back but are suffering with us. We aren't alone, abandoned. Someone or something we had is gone, but love has not gone, and we can let in the comfort of that love. God is suddenly powerful, not as a cosmic manipulator but as a comforting presence, and we can trust that comfort. We can even trust that what has happened will turn out fine after all. With this acceptance comes peace. We have not held anything back. We have struggled. We have felt deep feelings and expressed those feelings. The capacity to love is still ours, and now God— or just life's goodness—can be embraced with that same love. The pain of loss is lifted away, and we might even be blessed with a new freedom and more of a capacity for life than we had before.

Now all five stages were dangling in front of the group like a string of photographs from a wallet, and the grim picture that had begun had given way to a dramatically beautiful one. Yet, I had two final points to make:

a. People don't move neatly from stage to stage. On any given day we may spend time in any of the stages, in any order. The heart has its own logic and rhythm of healing that is impossible to predict accurately. All we can do is let ourselves respond and move with the response, wherever it leads. In order to complete our grief-work, we have to spend a certain amount of time in nearly all the five stages, until the job is done. It may take months and months. It depends on the loss. But with the guideposts of the grief-work map, we will be able to recognize our progress and always have hope.

b. Grief-work often depends on the availability of good, loving listeners. We need to be able to tell someone how sad, mad, or numb we are feeling. And that someone needs to understand grieving well enough not to interfere in our grief process with well-meant but badly timed advice. What we need from them is quite simple: "I'm here—do you want to talk?" All it takes is the wisdom to stay present and to keep caring.

The Witness

At this point, with the road map of grieving all laid out, I called upon Annette to tell her story. Rather than a formal witness talk, I interviewed Annette for about ten minutes in talk-show fashion. My asking her questions also modeled the kind of active listening a grieving person needs. The interview format allowed her to be free of the pressure to do an organized presentation and free to respond from the heart. In fact, Annette told me afterward that her witnessing in this fashion allowed her to go a step deeper in her acceptance. The questions I used to interview her are the following:

- Please sketch the basic facts—who was the person you lost, and what happened?
- How long did it take you to work through the effects his death had on you?
- What kinds of feelings did you have during that period?
- What effect did all those feelings have on your faith?
- What kind of response from others helped you most?
- What advice do you have for people who have to face a serious loss?

The Response Dialog

Next I invited the group members to talk in pairs about Annette's story, the five stages, and what they personally had gained so far in the workshop. Then after five minutes (or just enough time to get people in touch with what had been stirred in them), I brought the dialog back to the large group—about twenty people that night—and we listened to one another's stories about our own losses. The sharing had a gentle intensity—occasionally tearful and very satisfying. The young people had been freed up—they could now talk about significant deaths or other losses in their life. It was as if Kübler-Ross's wisdom and Annette's courage had woven among us a safe feeling about the worst thing in the world. Terrible losses had come to some and would surely come to all of us at various times in our life, but we knew now that we would be all right. Something far greater than the dreaded pain of loss would bring us through.

We felt what Saint Paul meant in Rom. 8:38–39, "For I am convinced that neither death nor life, . . . neither the present nor the future, nor any powers, neither height nor depth, nor anything else in all creation, will be able to separate us from the love of God that is in Christ Jesus our Lord" (NIV).

12

Dating Dilemmas: Exploring the Ethics of Dating

The Problem

At one of our weekly leadership meetings, I commented that it seems like teens often get badly hurt in dating relationships, not from any bad intention, just from ignorance about how to treat people right when romantic feelings are involved. The young people agreed with me instantly. One person summed up the feeling: "You take a risk when you love. You make yourself vulnerable. And if someone is rotten to you, it could be a long time before you trust again."

After much discussion we came to the following conclusions about this problem: dating someone takes courage, getting close to them and developing the relationship takes courage, and breaking up with them also takes courage. Often these challenges are not handled very well or very fairly. We agreed that needless harm could be avoided if we could come up with some caring and honest ways to handle the challenges and changes inherent in dating relationships. But we are not trying to eliminate all of the pain of love—some pain can be a healthy part of growing up and should not be avoided. We're talking only about the unnecessary pain that comes from people being inconsiderate and unkind to one another.

The leadership group made a list of specific problem areas—"dating dilemmas"—in which people get mistreated and hurt. That list of situations was brought to the weekly youth meeting. We wanted everyone to go over the list, adding and subtracting items until we had a consensus on what our particular youth group considered to be the toughest dating dilemmas. An entire Sunday night meeting was needed to bring out all the different kinds of struggles people were facing and to complete the list.

I told the group that their list of dating dilemmas would be presented in this book, not as *the* list, but rather as an expression of what one youth group finds troublesome in the dating process. My purpose, and theirs, is to stimulate your group to make its own list and to set in motion your own process of talking, searching, and praying about these dilemmas.

In several later meetings we worked on solutions to the dilemmas. I have summarized these solutions and added them to our list of dilemmas. Again, our solutions are not to be taken as conclusive answers to the dating dilemmas of everyone in your group, but they can serve as points of comparison with the dilemmas and solutions your group may wish to develop.

Dating Dilemmas and Solutions

Our list of dilemmas and solutions breaks down into four distinct categories that are common aspects of dating relationships.

The "Getting Started" Aspect: Some Troublesome Attitudes

Dilemma 1: Someone asks you out on the basis of physical attraction; she or he expresses no interest in building a friendship.

Solution: Sometimes the best response is a firm "no thank you," but it depends on the person. Sometimes underneath the movement of physical attraction, a caring heart lies waiting to be uncovered. Even when physical attraction seems to be the primary motive, accepting one date and proposing the building of a friendship might be worth a try. When dating doesn't reach for friendship, it quickly breaks down. Friendship is the solid foundation for good dating relationships.

Dilemma 2: You want to have a girlfriend or a boyfriend as a convenience, like a car or a VCR, just because it's harder socially to be alone.

Solution: Treating a person like a possession is emotionally abusive. Fight it in yourself. Fight it in your partner. If convenience is the primary basis for a dating relationship, get out of it or you will both get hurt.

Dilemma 3: You are asked out by someone you're not interested in romantically, and you don't know how to be honest without rejecting the person.

Solution: Dating is a trial-and-error method of discovering the qualities (chemistry) that attract you to another person. But it's hard to discern qualities in another person from surface impressions. If you feel the person asking you out is a good human being, you can accept the date on a friendly basis, to find out whether the relationship feels right. If there's no special electricity, you should not accept a second date. And do not give any vague excuses (that's lying). Explain why you don't want to continue dating the person. For example: "I don't feel that continued dating is going to work out." That way you don't build false hopes. The truth spoken with real caring is freeing for everyone.

Dilemma 4: You are really down on yourself because you don't have a boyfriend or a girlfriend. You begin to feel that something must be wrong with you.

Solution: Equating your self-worth with your love life is a big mistake. There is a lot more to you and a lot more to life than being someone's partner. Let love come when and however it wishes, and remember that there is a lot of time ahead for that to happen. Your main concern right now is to keep on finding and bringing out more and more of the treasures that you are, and you can do this in all kinds of relationships, not just dating relationships. Do not fall into the trap of worshiping love. Put your trust in Jesus and in yourself.

The "Going Deeper" Aspect:
Some Troublesome Behavior

Dilemma 1: The person you're dating starts behaving in a way you dislike, but you don't want to offend her or him by saying something.

Solution: If your partner behaves in a way you feel is wrong, you'll be supporting the behavior if you don't speak up. True, it's a risk to bring the matter up. No matter how gently you express your feelings, you might scare the person away. But you also might open up a whole new trust because you cared enough and dared to speak. Don't worry about what might happen, speak up. Even if the behavior turns out to be harmless, a relationship that stifles honesty is worthless.

Dilemma 2: The person you're with won't open up, won't let you in on his or her real feelings, won't get close, and won't allow any communication to go beyond surface things.

Solution: Women especially complain that men won't open up their inner feelings and thoughts. But sometimes these same women are so busy expressing their feelings and thoughts that they don't really invite the men to share, they don't really offer a listening heart. A good way to initiate some sharing would be to ask, "How important is it to you whether we learn to get beyond surface communication?"

Dilemma 3: When something difficult happens between you and your partner, the other person turns off, or blows up, and won't talk about it.

Solution: Handling hurt when it comes from someone you care for is love's greatest challenge. People normally clam up or blow up. Pray first, to regain a positive attitude, then quietly state your feelings. After you have stated your feelings, ask a lot of questions and listen carefully to the other person. When both partners are believers, a time of hurt feelings is a good time to join hands and pray together.

Dilemma 4: The person you're dating doesn't respect your limits on how far to go sexually and just keeps pushing.

Solution: Every dating couple has to mutually agree to their limits regarding sexual activity, or the relationship will go sour. Disagreements must be worked out and agreements made, or an important part of dating will become a battle-ground that will erode otherwise-good feelings for each other. In making an agreement about the limits of sexual activity, both partners should be aware that "going all the way" in a dating relationship will undermine rather than enhance the growth of friendship, and it will make breaking up a great deal more painful, even personally destructive.

**The "Other People" Aspect:
Some Troublesome Questions**

Dilemma 1: How much should I tell a friend about what's happening between me and my girlfriend or boyfriend?

Solution: If your friend is trustworthy, you should feel free to tell him or her anything you want or need to. Confiding in a friend may be a necessary way to sort out your feelings about what is happening in the relationship and about how to proceed. Let your partner in on any conversations with other friends that involve him or her so that trust will be maintained and both of you can benefit from them.

Dilemma 2: What if my boyfriend or girlfriend gets possessive and becomes jealous of time spent with other friends or in activities that do not include him or her?

Solution: Possessiveness is selfish and destructive and should not be tolerated. Nip it in the bud, and if it continues to grow, end the relationship. A possessive or jealous person will deprive you of other relationships you need for growth. Possessiveness and jealousy are signs that love is lacking. A healthy love relationship has room for lots of other friendships.

Dilemma 3: How much should I let myself be influenced by what my friends think about my girlfriend or boyfriend?

Solution: Listen carefully to whatever your friends want to tell you. Then take it all to prayer, knowing that they may be way off base or they may be right on target. Ask Christ to show you which is the case, and only then draw your own conclusions.

Dilemma 4: What if my parents don't like my boyfriend or girlfriend?

Solution: Listen with an open mind to what your parents have to say. Some parents, whether from their own successes or their own failures in love, will have a lot of wisdom to offer you about your dating decisions. On the other hand, some parents might not be all that helpful if they cannot get beyond their own experience and see yours for what it is. In either case, ask them to stand beside you and coach you instead of trying to make your decisions for you. In some cases, your parents may see a danger that you don't and order you to break off the relationship. If this happens, you need to obey them because at high-school age, you're still under their authority. If you deeply feel they're wrong, go to God and put the matter in God's hands. Ask for the light to see the situation through God's eyes and the courage to do what is best for all involved.

The "Breaking Up" Aspect:
Some Troublesome Reactions

Dilemma 1: You've lost "that lovin' feeling," but you keep the relationship going because you don't want all the upset and hassle of breaking up.

Solution: The turmoil of breaking up is painful but healthy. Both partners are freed up to enter new dating relationships that can bring new growth. Most dating relationships have only so much to offer, and it's an act of kindness to say so when you realize it's time to move on.

Dilemma 2: You want to end the relationship, so you act cold and hope she or he "gets the picture."

Solution: The great majority of teen love relationships will break up. Breaking up is a normal process, so it's good to learn how. A well-handled breakup is talked out, not just acted out. In fact, a healthy breakup may take several long conversations. The more both partners understand each other, the freer it will leave them. During the breakup both partners need to share what they have gained from being together. If friendship was truly developed during the dating relationship, it will actually be strengthened by going through the pain of breaking up in a considerate and open way.

Dilemma 3: You're told "it's over," but you refuse to believe it and won't let go.

Solution: Refusing to let go when that's what the other person wants is selfishness. You will only do harm to yourself and your partner by hanging on. If your attachment feels like a life-or-death loss, pray about the situation and ask Christ to take you beyond it. He will see you through the sadness and help you to make new beginnings.

Dilemma 4: At the worst possible time and in the worst possible place, you get the bad news that your partner wants out.

Solution: The reason nearly all teen romantic relationships break up is that both partners, at this age, still have a lot to learn about love. So even at the beginning, expect that the dating relationship may well break up. When the time comes, if you feel and know that the relationship is over, choose a time and place free from a lot of other pressures—a time and place where both of you can freely air all the feelings involved and be able to leave the relationship behind with hope, confidence, and a good feeling about each other.

Again, this list of dilemmas and solutions is offered not as your list or your solutions but rather as a stimulus for dialog. For it is in dialog within the group that the dilemmas get named and the solutions get realistically explored.

I will close with two Gospel verses that seem to shed light on the search for solutions to dating dilemmas. The first passage is, "'Do to others as you would have them do to you'" (Luke 6:31, NIV). In romantic relationships we can be tempted to act selfishly because our needs, our feelings, and our very hope of happiness seem to be on the line. But our actual happiness also depends on caring deeply about the effects our decisions have on others as well as ourselves. The second passage is, "'. . . The truth will set you free'" (John 8:32, NIV). When strong feelings are involved, like those in a dating relationship, we can be tempted to withhold the truth because the truth sometimes hurts. But if expressed with love, the truth opens the way for the communication and the learning that are necessary for personal growth and lasting healthy relationships.

13

I Can't Go On:
Suicide-proofing Young People

An astonishing 73 percent of American teens have thought seriously about killing themselves ("Teenagers Think About Suicide," *Group* 15 [September 1987]: 21). Most of that thinking is done alone, some of it gets shared with peers, and only rarely is it shared with an adult. Clearly this is an issue that requires careful attention in our ministries to youth.

The experts in pastoral care for suicidal persons in the Boston area are called the *Samaritans*. They operate a twenty-four-hour suicide hot line, with a separate number for teen callers who can talk with peer counselors called the *Samariteens*. In addition to their suicide hot line, the Samaritans help train people to spot and respond to the warning signals in someone with suicidal feelings. Their message goes out to young people in schools and churches through pamphlets and guest speakers.

The wisdom of the Samaritans' approach is that when people are coached to attend to the trouble signs in friends and loved ones, they are also being trained in how to respond to their own times of depression. The approach amounts to a kind of suicide-proofing.

The Samaritans' excellent publications and a list of comparable hot lines throughout the country can be obtained by sending five dollars to The Samaritans, 500 Commonwealth Avenue, Boston, MA 02125. There is also a national teen suicide hot line at 1-800-621-4000, a good number to hand out to your group.

In this chapter, I share a method our group discovered, almost by accident, for opening up this highly charged area of teen thinking to let in a little of Christ's light and love.

Our youth group decided to join two other groups in planning a Sunday afternoon of games, a liturgy, an evening cookout, and a fellowship time. Our group was asked to plan the fellowship time—a time for sharing. Gina, a member of our youth group, volunteered a short skit she had written about suicide. "Suicide is a topic a lot of people can relate to," Gina explained. The plan looked good. The groups would watch the skit, have a discussion, and then pray together about the issues and concerns that people raised in the discussion.

Soon the big day had arrived and everything was going according to plan. The games proved to be quite competitive and a lot of fun. The Mass and the cookout were warm and relaxing. We all looked forward to the fellowship time, during which we would have the opportunity to open up and get to know one another on a deeper level.

The skit was simple—one story, acted out twice with a different ending each time. Here's the scenario:

A teenage girl sits down and then gets up and starts pacing around the room. She then sits down again, alone and sad. She says, "No one cares, no one understands." She reveals a large bottle of pills. The phone rings but she will not answer it. Instead, she swallows the pills and dies. Then the caller is heard recording this message: "Jill, I just want you to know that if you ever need to talk, I'll be there." End of version one.

In version two, the same girl, in the same mood, with the same bottle of pills, says again, "No one cares. No one understands." While she's holding up the pills and staring at them, the doorbell rings. She hides the pills, answers the door, and lets in a very upset friend, who says, "Jill, I need to talk. I'm so confused, and I'm hurting so bad. I can't talk to most people about how I feel, but I felt I could talk to you." Then she just cries and Jill holds her. After a while she says,

"Thanks, Jill, for listening and letting me cry on your shoulder. It is so good to have a friend who cares. You've helped me a lot."

Jill responds, "But you've helped me too, more than you know!" The friend leaves, and Jill throws the bottle of pills out the window. End of version two.

After two of our group members had finished performing both versions of the skit, silence filled the room. Then someone said quietly, "That could have been me." Gina, the young woman who had written the skit, responded, "That was me about a year ago, but please don't tell my parents, it would worry them too much." Someone else said, "My best friend committed suicide last year, and I've been closing out everyone ever since." He wept as he said it, and soon arms were around his shoulders on both sides. Gina and one of the actors then mentioned, "We realized when we were doing this skit that trusting someone is the answer."

Gradually, more and more people talked about how suicide had touched them, either as a temptation or by the suicide of a loved one. Someone commented, "When you are depressed it is hard to see, but to kill yourself is to kill something in every person who loves you." Someone else said, "You get so caught up in yourself that you can't see the love others have for you." Another person added, "One time when I was really down, I talked to a friend, and he just felt helpless. But when I talked it all out with Jesus, I felt a peace come over me."

The openness that flowed through the group was like a healing, refreshing bath. We adults felt privileged to be there. And what was quite amazing to all of us was that for the most part, these were wholesome, capable teens. We would never have guessed that they carried such dark feelings about life within them.

We closed the evening, as our group normally does, by dimming the lights, putting on gentle music, and giving everyone a chance to pray with someone else. For a number of the young people, this was the first time they had opened up to Christ in prayer and felt the power of his love. For all of us, it was a time to know with renewed clarity how much hidden hurt our teens carry around with them and how deeply runs their need for Jesus as a friend they can turn to.

"'Come to me, all who labor and are heavy laden, and I will give you rest. Take my yoke upon you, and learn from me; for I am gentle and lowly in heart, and you will find rest for your souls. For my yoke is easy, and my burden is light'" (Matt. 11:28–30, RSV). That was Jesus' message to the young people that night.

After that meeting, one young woman who had been secretly suicidal for months went home, wrote a suicide note, and left it out for her parents to find. She did not attempt suicide but used the note as the most direct way she could manage to signal her distress. Therapy, which she freely accepted, began shortly after.

At our own youth meeting a few weeks later, our group had a discussion about suicide that was less personal and emotional; it was more a surfacing of questions about what happens after death. "Does God forgive suicide?" someone asked. By way of answer, I told them what I had read about people who have had the experience of being clinically dead and leaving their bodies but then have been resuscitated. They all reported sadness at coming back because of the peace they felt in the "next world"—*except for those who had attempted suicide.* These people were glad to be alive again because waiting for them was a long period of terrible distress during which they would feel all the pain and damage to others that their own suicide would have caused. (For more information about after-death experiences, see Raymond Moody's book *Life After Life* [New York: Bantam Books, 1975].)

The possibility of such distress after suicide sharply undercuts any romantic illusions young people may harbor about suicide being a final release from trouble. A shocking perspective, but it removes some of the glamour and attraction suicide can have for some people. I offer it along with the skit, discussion, and prayer approach as an additional technique you may want to use in your efforts to suicide-proof your young people.

Whatever approach you decide to use to suicide-proof your youth, make sure it includes creating conditions in which young people can talk freely. A listening, caring atmosphere is the most powerful tool we have for healing the hurts that prompt thoughts of suicide.

14

When I Was Hungry: Planning Service to Poor People

Half of the world's people, nearly 2.5 billion, live in countries where the annual per capita income is four hundred dollars or less. At least 800 million people in those countries live in absolute poverty. Nearly half a billion people are chronically hungry, despite abundant harvests worldwide (*Origins* 16 [27 November 1986]: 436). Several corresponding facts about world hunger really seem to hit home with young people. Sixty-seven percent of the world's people are hungry right now, and they must live in chronic undernourishment. About forty thousand people die each day of starvation—that equals twenty-eight people a minute, or one every two to three seconds ("Love Loaf News," Hunger Fact Sheet, World Vision, 1988).

Youth do stop, listen, and let the awfulness of these statistics stun them for the duration of a discussion, but then their hearts move on to other more immediate concerns. They do care and don't mean to turn away from this tragedy, but it's hard to sustain care for people you don't know and can't see.

How do we awaken our young people to the global reality of hunger without shocking them into either denial or guilt but not so cautiously as to let them just roll over and switch channels? Young people need more than the impact of statistics if they are to empathize with the desperation of 67 percent of their brothers and sisters. They need some first-hand experience of the desperate condition so that when they are adult Catholics, hungry poor people will have a real place in their prayers, their giving, their voting, and their hearing of the Gospel.

This chapter describes three projects we found effective in enabling young people to act on behalf of hungry people. The projects were not directed to hungry poor people living in far-off third world countries but rather to people living across economic borders that are quite near. Instead of allowing the problem of world hunger to remain distant and abstract, our strategy was to make it as close and concrete, and hence as manageable, as the giving of a cup of water.

Project 1: Soup Kitchen

Soup kitchens have sprung up all over the United States in recent years, due to the surge of North American homelessness and poverty. Many soup kitchens are organized and operated in such a way that responsibilities are rotated among groups from churches, clubs, schools, and even businesses. Our youth group recently was given a Monday night slot every few months in the schedule of a busy Episcopalian soup kitchen. Our mission was to first cook and bring, and then to heat and serve, 225 dinners to the hungry people of downtown Boston.

Our effort was headed up by a high school senior working with one college-age adult and a team of five other planners. They mobilized the cooking efforts of about forty-four parish families and the serving efforts of about fifteen adventuresome group members.

The bags, cans, and coolers of food were gathered and loaded into our cars. When everything was loaded and ready, we stood in a circle and prayed with great anxiety and excitement. We asked for extra helpings of love to take with us.

When we got to Saint John the Evangelist Church, we hit the ground running. There were tables to set, salads to serve, casseroles to heat, and so on. The work went on at a frantic pace. The guests were not-so-patiently waiting, and soon the platefuls of good food were pouring out of the kitchen at amazing speeds. There were many grateful and affirming comments, some obnoxious and demanding comments, several tender moments, and a few difficult moments. All in all, it was a challenging night.

When the last guest was gone and the last bit of cleanup was complete, we sat in a circle and debriefed. The young people freely shared their reflections and reactions:

- "They looked normal."
- "They looked so sad."
- "I loved it."
- "I was scared."
- "I got proposed to."
- "I got pinched."
- "I feel funny going back to a home where I have everything I need."
- "I feel grateful going back to a home where I have everything I need."

Serving that meal was a first for us. In three months we will get another slot, and we really want it. More of the group wants to be involved the next time. The experience really affected the whole group; it impacted our hearts. The impacts were heavy but healthy.

We've been slow in building service outreach into the rhythm of our youth ministry activities. Perhaps because helping the teens get their life and their faith together has been so time- and attention-consuming. But a change has definitely come. Youth community outreach to people in distress can no longer be an occasional extra for us. Having experienced it, we now feel and know that a necessary part of our Christian identity as a group and as individuals is completed this way. How can we say that we know and love Jesus if we do not serve him by serving the needs of our most vulnerable sisters and brothers?

Project 2: Habitat for Humanity

A second form of outreach to poor people has also recently become available to our youth group. A group called "Habitat for Humanity" is building homes for low-income families in Lawrence (a city near us) and in 250 or so other cities across the country. The group uses donated property, labor, and funds to build (or rebuild) homes for struggling families who can buy them, without down payments and interest, in monthly mortgage payments that are well below rental rates.

We've been up to the work site in Lawrence eight times. Twice we stayed overnight in donated accommodations. Lunch was provided by other volunteer church groups.

The work was good for us. We got close to people of all ages, people with southern, western, and eastern accents. We met believers of every kind, as well as nonbelievers who chose to help out of their own goodwill. Germans, Cambodians, and Hispanics, some of them soon to occupy these homes, all worked together. Everyone was happy and grateful to work hard for something so good. People got very close. Good-byes were tearful.

So far, only a small number of our teens have dared to pick up a hammer and put out a long day or two; building homes involves a bit more time and sweat than does working in a soup kitchen. But the flavor of the stories coming back is positive and is spreading. I believe the number of volunteers from our youth community will increase in the future.

Both of these outreaches have posed a much-needed spiritual challenge to our youth group. Previously, the spiritual emphasis of the youth community often had provided a challenge for the receptive, more relational dimension of faith life that can be more attractive to girls than boys. That challenge goes something like this: "Open up and let one another in and let Christ in. Get close to him and close to one another. Say what you feel; help create a place of caring and joy!" That's a challenge to the inner person, one that I have found young women, to their credit, handle better than young men. But faith has another side, an action side, a challenge to the outer person that young men find especially attractive: "Raft that river, ski that mountain," but stronger yet, "Build that house, serve that junkie from the streets."

If I am about to be charged with flagrant sexism, let me say quickly that both sexes need both types of challenges, and a balanced youth group with a balanced spirituality will find ways to issue both challenges loud and clear. In our parish, I now see young men and young women quietly challenging one another's courage. For example: "Are you going up to Habitat?" or "Are you going to the next soup kitchen?" And I see a different kind of look on the faces of the young people who have not joined our youth community yet. It is not a "scorn for the church" look but an "I don't quite dare to yet" look. And I must admit, I like the clear message that it takes a certain kind of gutsiness to be a member of the group. Actually, it takes an equal amount of courage to let the power of God in as it does to let it out. And having both parts of the picture strongly represented in the events we run balances the two faith challenges just right.

Project 3: Collections for the Needy

Another kind of service project that is ideally suited for parish teens is collecting goods no longer being used, which families have stowed away in an attic or a closet just in case they need them "someday." We did two of these collections. One collection was for a church with a special ministry to its ethnic immigrant population. They needed and we provided a huge amount of children's clothing. The other was for a group that helps homeless families get a new start. They needed and we provided a huge amount of household furnishings. Both of the collections were effective and enjoyable. Here is how they worked.

Collecting Used Clothing

Our youth group got a call from an inner-city parish that serves a community from the Cape Verde Islands. They needed children's clothing. "How much do you need?" I asked. "You can't bring us too much," I was told by Father Leo. "We'll see about that," I said. And this became our challenge: "We'll show him." It was early December, just the right season for the project.

We got the whole parish into the effort, digging clothes out of attics, cellars, and closets—clothes that had been outgrown but were too nice to throw away. Youth group members hit up their families and friends. Parishioners did the same. We placed huge boxes in the hallways of the parish center. Each box was labeled with an age-group and a clothing type. Volunteers sorted the clothes for us when people dropped them off. As a box got full, we taped it up, labeled it, and set it aside. And the boxes did get full. A landslide of clothing came pouring in. In the end, three vans were loaded to the roof with boxes and delivered to Father Leo. I will always treasure the dropped jaw and the overwhelmed expression on his face as thirty big, heavy boxes were lugged into his meeting room. "We'll let people send some of this back to their families on the islands," he said in a stunned tone. We got him good.

Collecting Furniture and Household Goods

The other project came to us by way of Shawn, a youth community alumnus who had gotten involved with the Massachusetts Coalition for the Homeless. (Similar coalitions exist all over the United States, and they all have a similar need—furnishings for families making a new start.) Shawn, now studying for a doctorate in theology, wondered if his old youth group could help this organization he had come to love.

First, we invited Shawn to come and talk to us about homelessness. He did a good job of opening our eyes and minds. "In 1974, there were 250,000 homeless people in the United States. In 1984, there were two million. By the year 2000, if the current trend continues, there will be nineteen million." (Shawn's data came from a National Housing Fact Sheet distributed by the Massachusetts Coalition for the Homeless.) The strength of his talk convinced us to put a notice in the church bulletin and the local newspaper:

When a homeless family starts over . . .
WE CAN HELP!
This Saturday, 12 November, please bring your presently unused furniture and household goods
to the parish center between 10 a.m. and 2 p.m.,
or call the rectory for a pick up.

A crew of about a dozen teens worked nonstop for those four hours, unloading the parade of cars that came or trucking things to the parish center from people's homes. The work was bone-wearying but exhilarating, and it resulted in a mountain of stuff. And it was good stuff; much of it looked new. We had collected everything a family might need for their home. The Coalition had to make two trips with their moving van to cart it all away.

The collection for the Coalition for the Homeless worked so well that it's being publicized among other youth groups. You can get the name and number of the homeless advocacy group in your state by calling directory assistance.

Both times that we gathered goods for poor people, the sense of joy and energy released reached the same incredible high. After a day of moving furniture, one young person said, "Guys, this is unbelievable. I feel so good. I truly didn't want to come. It was all *should*. But I had the best time. This was great."

There's a mystery here. Just when an effort looks like it will be boring and hard and no fun at all, we find an amazing emotional payoff.

Maybe it's the law of Karma, "'. . . The measure you give will be the measure you get . . .'" (Mark 4:24, RSV). We're giving a lot, so we get a lot back.

"'When you give a feast, invite the poor, the maimed, the lame, the blind, and you will be blessed, because they cannot repay you . . .'" (Luke 14:13–14, RSV). Maybe that blessing just comes very quickly.

Maybe "faith by itself, if it is not accompanied by action, is dead" (James 2:17, NIV). It surely does seem to me that a youth group is only as alive as it is generous. Or to put it another way, a combined effort to give of themselves brings on a surge of group vitality.

Or maybe it's even simpler: "'For I was hungry and you gave me food . . .'" (Matt. 25:35, RSV). How could doing a direct act of kindness to Christ himself *not* be tremendously satisfying? And whether we recognize Christ in those we serve or not, he says that he really is there, and the joy we feel is the clue that confirms his presence.

15

When I Was Old: Planning Service to Senior Citizens

This chapter offers three program ideas for outreach to the elderly that have proven to be lots of fun for both young and old. But before presenting these ideas, I want to describe a school-based youth ministry in Jamaica that gave us two key ingredients in our group's outreach recipe.

My friend Fr. Simon Harak ran that youth ministry, which consisted entirely of service outreach. The young people went to orphanages, hospitals, prisons, and nursing homes. Here's the pattern they used: The group would first meet and talk briefly to re-establish the Matt. 25:35 perspective—"'When I was sick . . . in prison . . . a stranger,'" and so forth. They would pray together for the people awaiting their visits and then go their separate ways to serve Jesus in his various disguises. Their mission was to bring aid and comfort in any way they could but also to always include somewhere in the visit, if ever so briefly, a moment of prayer with the persons to whom they ministered. Sharing prayer was awkward at first, but soon it became an accepted practice.

Afterward, the young people would gather at their meeting place, tell their stories, and discern what God had done through them and how it had matched up to the Scriptures. They finished with prayer and thanks.

And that was their program—no dances, no beach trips, nothing else—just several groups of young people (totaling about 120 students) doing real ministry week after week and loving it.

Three years after Father Simon had come back to the United States, he received startling news from Jamaica. Nine young men from his youth ministry program wanted to become priests. Father Simon said, "They had experienced what great things the Spirit could do through them. After that, having tasted the joys of ministry firsthand, why wouldn't they want to make a life of it?"

The story of Father Simon's ministry and those vocations goaded me from the time I first heard it. Our youth group normally prayed before we did things, but to pray with the people we visited and then to debrief thoroughly right afterward—these were new ingredients. Now, having tried these ingredients, I am happy to announce that they do indeed add good flavor to the outreach ministry our group has established with senior citizens.

Program Idea 1: Intergenerational Luncheon

The intergenerational luncheon has become an annual tradition for us over the last eleven years. Cathy and Sandy, two senior girls, created the event to reach out and try to combat the loneliness suffered by some of our elder parishioners. The luncheon is a fall or spring event put on by the youth group for their grandparents' generation. The Christian service commission of the parish funds the event. The teens decorate and prepare a big room in the parish center, and cook and serve a festive meal. Youth group members join with the elders at all the tables so both generations can eat and socialize together.

The meal is only the start of the party. After everyone has finished eating and the dishes have been cleared away, the young people introduce some of their favorite youth community songs—both the crazy ones and the devotional ones. Then a skit, chosen mostly for its comic value, is performed.

After the skit, intergenerational sharing begins. At each table people begin conversations using the same kinds of get-acquainted questions that we use in our meetings. For example:

- What's your favorite movie (song, ice cream, month) and why?
- Who in your life most influenced your faith?
- Tell about the first time you kissed a member of the other sex.
- What means the most to you about this parish?

The alternating hilarity and intensity of the discussions is a delight to all.

Finally, we do an old-fashioned sing-along, using songs like "When the Saints Go Marching In," "You Are My Sunshine," "It's a Grand Old Flag," and so on. The last song is always "Amazing Grace."

The event concludes with spontaneous prayers of the faithful. Both young and old are familiar and comfortable with this form of prayer because that's how our parish prays at Mass. Since we've been closing the festivities this way, these prayers have become the climactic moment of the day. Great affection, great joy, new respect, and heartfelt gratitude pour forth. The feeling as people leave and afterward as we debrief about the event is, invariably, exhilaration.

The other two events I offer are not yet perennials—we've done each of them once—but the joy they generated was comparable to the intergenerational luncheon. Thus, they will likely get into our annual rotation of favorite activities. The events grew out of a now-discontinued custom of Christmas caroling at several senior citizen housing developments. We had begun to feel frustrated with the remoteness of just singing for people and moving on without a chance to make more contact. So David, a creative senior, proposed a new kind of Christmas outreach.

Program Idea 2: Epiphany Talent Show

We contacted the community council at Peter Sanborn Place, a local retirement residence, and proposed a joint Epiphany celebration between their community and our youth community. Because Epiphany is about the three kings bringing gifts, we suggested that everyone be invited to come and honor Christ by giving one another gifts originating from their talents—perhaps by reading a favorite poem, playing an instrument, singing a song, telling a story, or performing a skit. Teens and elders would share these kinds of gifts with one another and then have refreshments together. The community council agreed to the proposal.

A letter went out to all the residents and all the youth group members, and posters advertising the event were posted. The young people created a Christmas fireplace and placed a big armchair on one side of it for the gift givers and a manger scene on the other side. For their contribution, the elders brought plates full of sweet delicacies. About ten different talents were slated to be presented.

Setting the scene took a while, and when everything and everyone was finally in place, we noticed that the two generations were sitting in separate areas like shy junior high students at a dance. David, the young master of ceremonies, and I stood up and announced to everyone:

> Folks, we have a problem. Because this evening is all about friendship and sharing between the generations, the show cannot go on until this segregated seating situation is changed into a thorough blend. And on the way to a new seat, everyone must meet at least three members of the other generation.

Amid laughter, people went about the mixing, and the mood for David's opening prayer was already upbeat. We all joined hands for the prayer.

The gifts of talents people brought to one another were simple and satisfying. Most of them were from the youth community, two of them were from the residents. Several people sang songs expressing love and gratitude to Christ, others shared their favorite reading, and still others gave musical performances on instruments such as the guitar, the piano, the harmonica, and the fiddle. The talent sharing closed with a youth community tradition—the reading of an abridged version of Henry Van Dyke's *The Story of the Other Wise Man* (New York: Harper and Row, 1896).

As refreshments were being served, the senior citizens expressed their amazement at the teens' openness, joy, goodness, and faith. "We hadn't seen these qualities in teens for a while," they said. "We didn't know they still existed."

Afterward, at the debriefing, the sense of having given a significant gift was felt by all the young people, but they also felt frustration at the reticence of the elders to share their talents and gifts. This frustration led to the next event for elders, which is described in the following section.

Program Idea 3: Story Sharing

This event was scheduled for Easter time. Again, we waited a week or two after Easter so more people would be available. Our intent was to have an evening just to swap stories between the generations. The purpose was to allow a more free-flowing exchange, with no need to perform. A kind of "hanging out together" was intended, with just enough preparation to give direction.

We sent a letter to every resident, saying that we wanted to come visit them again to get to know them better. We invited both elders and teens to bring stories—funny stories, stories about how things used to be, personal faith stories, and stories about life-changing experiences.

Because witnessing faith stories was a normal part of our youth meetings, we asked the young people to bring those faith stories that had gone over well at our meetings.

The big night came, and we were in for a disappointment. Forty people had come to the Epiphany event, over half of the residents. This time only about a dozen showed up. "What happened?" we asked. The response was, "Well, the letter came over a week ago, and people just tend to forget. And you didn't put up a poster this time." Well, live and learn, but here we were. And there was once again an abundance of those sweet treats to console us in our disappointment. And besides, about fifteen young people were present so that meant the age-groups were pretty evenly matched.

Long tables were arranged in a big square so that people were facing each other, and the treats were laid out in front of us. We began with an opening prayer, praying that everyone would feel at ease in sharing their stories, and then said, "Ready, set, go!" Several teens started, then several elders, then several more teens, and the exchange rolled along with great gusto. We heard stories from ski trips and from the workplace. We heard about potential fight situations handled with prayer. And we heard stories about learning to milk cows, about what downtown Reading used to look like, about what I did to the car the first time I took it out alone, and about the temptation to use drugs. We heard school stories and love stories and yes, a few good faith stories. Many laughs and a lot of drama emerged from the things we told one another. The story swapping went on nonstop for about an hour and fifteen minutes, and then we closed it with the Lord's Prayer and said good night.

Several new elements seemed to emerge in this event. People of both generations experienced spontaneous exchange for the first time, and they were delighted to have

been part of it. For the young people, their stereotype of "the old person" gave way to a recognition of distinct personalities:
- "This one is such a character."
- "That one had such a short fuse."
- "This one was really into what we were saying."
- "That one is such a love."

And for the older people, a kind of compassionate shock wave hit them as they picked up on the kind of pace, pressures, and problems today's youth have to cope with. The teens felt that they had really been heard and understood. When we debriefed afterward, we concluded that the smaller numbers actually contributed to the more intimate experience we enjoyed together.

Youth outreach to the elderly has a strong mutual benefit. At the same time that our society is isolating our elders in gray ghettos that can become places of sadness and loneliness, our youth are suffering from a similar kind of inattention—with both parents working and grandparents often far away. Each of these generations has its own particular sadness, which contact with one another can alleviate.

The three events described in this chapter are all satisfying to do, but they are only experimental probes—we've just gotten a toe in the water. I'm glad to report that the water, so far, is fine. But what remains to be discovered is a workable way to keep alive and growing the intergenerational relationships that have just begun. Matt. 25:35 spurs us on, for the distress in the Body of Christ calls out to us from both generations. And it seems quite likely that great joys await youth ministries that answer that call.

Part B
Inviting
the Divine

"The essence of Christian faith is a living relationship with God . . ." (*The Challenge of Adolescent Catechesis: Maturing in Faith* [Washington, DC: National Federation for Catholic Youth Ministry, 1986], p. 4). But just as we can find or lose touch with—even bury—our own human selves, we also can find or lose touch with—even shut out—the God who loves us. And that loss of a sense of God now threatens the adolescents of the nineties. A generation is coming of age with a great spiritual deficit.

The Catholic church in the United States has responded to this threat. *A Vision of Youth Ministry* (Washington, DC: USCC, 1976) established for the eighties the great necessity of a person-centered approach to young people. Now, in the nineties, *The Challenge of Adolescent Catechesis* has called for an explicitly Christ-centered approach so that our young people can grow up in a "living relationship" with their God.

Perhaps the challenge within the challenge is offering a catechesis that not only brings the human and the Divine together, but does it in a way that also communicates a personal spirituality and a Catholic identity. Recent youth work in the Catholic church has often been far too cautious about offering a catechesis that employs the traditional Catholic ways for inviting Christ into our human experience. We have edged away from such things as the rosary, the sacraments, fasting, and daily prayer—probably fearing that the old traditions would bring along with them the old person-burying spirituality of a church we still remember all too well.

Consequently, the chapters in this part of the book explore what a Christ-centered catechesis that employs many Catholic traditions for meeting Christ can do for the personal growth of young people. My personal experience is that the fresh discovery of our Catholic traditions of prayer actually produces delight in young people—not defeating, but greatly promoting, the personal freedom and wholeness we so fiercely covet for them.

In addition, the strategies presented in the following chapters are designed to get both generations talking about and tasting the good things that belong to us by way of our inheritance as Catholic Christians and, in doing so, to find Christ in things very Catholic.

Therefore, the premise that underlies the second part of this book is as follows:

> Adolescence is the dawning time of firsthand discovery of God. If, as adults, we will throw off our inhibitions about our Catholic tradition and share our personal experience of the treasures of our amazing heritage, young people will catch our enthusiasm. They will then quite readily discover in their own church the prayer practices they need to bring Christ into their personal life. And, in doing so, they will also take their rightful places in the unfolding identity of the two-thousand-year-old Catholic Christian community.

16
Pass the Candle:
Venturing into Spiritual Openness

A lot of adults do not think so, but our young people have a hearty appetite for spirituality. To put it more bluntly, there's a hunger for God gnawing at many of our young people, and as adults, we often frustrate that hunger because we do not know it is there.

I have heard many adult youth leaders say, "Religion turns kids off, you have to focus on fun and enthusiasm." Well, you can do that, and you should, because fun and enthusiasm are real needs too. But the deeper longing in the majority of young people lies in the realm of spirituality and faith. Young people everywhere are searching for meaning and joy, intensity and peace. And while this search can lead to destruction, it can just as often lead to Christ.

Let me illustrate my claim with a technique we have used dozens of times to great effect. We call it "pass the candle." The technique came to us from the Teen Encounter program at Saint Basil's in Methuen, Massachusetts. Where they got it I do not know, but it's one of our beloved prayer methods.

To begin, everyone sits in a circle, and someone turns off the lights. The leader lights a candle and explains:

> The candle will be passed around from person to person. When you receive it, you may share a thought, a prayer, or just hold it in silence. While you are holding the candle, the rest of us will focus our prayers and our thoughts on you and silently join you in what you say or pray.

Then the leader prays for the presence of the Spirit to move freely among the group. Next, people begin to pass the candle, at a slow pace, around the circle. To close, the leader may share a scriptural passage or a prayer of thanks.

The atmosphere of reverence for one another and for Christ that develops during this simple prayer service is a delight to experience. Some people will choose to remain silent, but I've found that even in the most inexperienced group, the longing to open up and spiritually draw close to one another will melt the inhibitions. People pray for loved ones, give thanks for things, share what the group means to them, or pray for what the group needs. No one gets bored. The sight of the moving candle and the sound of the heartfelt prayers capture everyone. Faith is the heart's deepest dimension, and we long to meet one another there.

So where did we get the impression that teens are turned off when things get spiritual? Mostly, I think, as a result of our own fear of sharing our faith. We may never have been invited to open up our own inner life of faith; thus, we may tend to resist sharing what touches us deeply and personally. Instead, the way we talk about our God is impersonal, doctrinal, preachy, and formal, and yes, that does turn off young people. Certainly there is a place for talking with youth about Christian doctrines, but that's not the place to start. The place to start is with firsthand experience of spiritual realities. Sharing firsthand spiritual experiences will generate the burning questions that lead later into good discussions of Christian doctrines and principles.

This approach to spirituality takes catechesis out of the realm of secondhand knowledge and makes it a matter of interpreting firsthand experience and then linking it up and verifying it with knowledge and wisdom couched in the language of our traditions. Now our catechesis can fulfill the classic definition of theology—*fides quaerens intellectum*, or "faith seeking understanding." That formula seems to capture just

how teens grow spiritually, and adults as well. First comes our
hunger for moments of real encounter with Christ, which
invites faith. Then and only then is born the second spiritual
appetite—figuring out what it all means, which prompts a
search for understanding. Youth ministry is most effective
when it assists in the satisfaction of both hungers, so that
both head and heart can become fully alive. ". . . 'You shall
love the Lord your God with all your heart and . . . with all
your mind'" (Matt. 22:37, RSV). These are not two isolated
areas to develop but the left and the right hand (or brain) of a
whole spirituality.

17
Our Own Mass: Activating Youth Worship

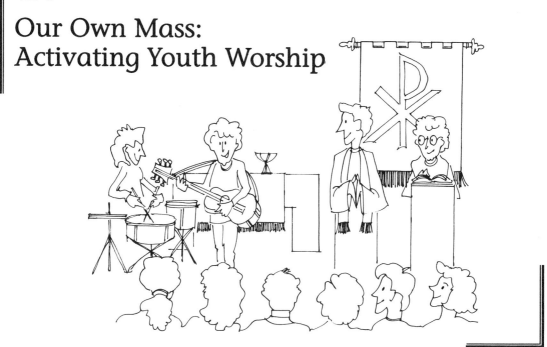

We are a TV generation, and this affects the way we behave at church. We easily fall into passively watching and listening to the Mass, waiting to see if anything will happen to excite us. If we adults have to work at rousing ourselves out of TV passivity when we worship, it is twice as hard for young people, who are much more deeply conditioned by the one-way media. "I didn't get anything out of Mass," is the common refrain. Many young people do not realize that Mass is not a show.

But young people *can* break out of an audience mentality and become involved worshipers who find in the Eucharist a great opportunity to open up and free up their inner self. Young people can make the change from passive mode to active mode in the way they worship. And by much trial and error, our youth community has developed a method of going to Mass that helps it happen. But before I describe our approach, allow me to tell a story that illustrates the kind of personal engagement in worship we promote.

Although she had attended Catholic schools all her life, Claudia had not had much experience in going to Mass. But then she met Lee, a young man from our youth group, and for him going to Mass was a great thing. So Lee took this novice worshiper by the hand and introduced her to our method of bringing our life and especially our struggles right into the liturgy and looking for Christ's response there.

On the day her grandmother died, Claudia really needed our method for worshiping. She arrived at the church in a panic, not over the death, which had been a long time coming and was much expected, but over her own total lack of feeling about this enormous loss. Claudia's grandmother had meant so much to her, and now she was appalled at the coldness she found in herself; she felt no sadness, just blankness.

Claudia went into a pew, got down on her knees, and asked Jesus to please help her find her heart and restore her love for her grandmother. That was her silent prayer all through the liturgy. When Claudia received communion, Christ answered her prayer. She felt his love fill her, and then gently the blessed weeping began—and kept on and on. Long after Mass was over, Claudia sat in that pew with Lee's arm around her, Christ's love within her, and tears of grateful grieving flowing freely.

Communion really took place for Claudia that day. She gave herself to Christ just as she was, and Christ gave himself to her just the way she needed him. But this communion did not just happen. Good preparation made the healing moment possible. Claudia was putting into practice certain simple and learnable principles of worship, which she had picked up from Lee and the youth group.

The worship approach we teach has two distinct and complementary dimensions: the personal and the communal. Mass is surely an individual and private experience with Christ, and it is just as surely a social and shared experience with Christ. Healthy worship integrates both dimensions. In our training for Mass, we open up the personal dimension and the communal dimension in two distinct kinds of preparation:

a. We help young people get personal in their worship through a carefully directed group dialog that invites sharing about what is or is not going on for each of us at Mass.

b. We help young people get free in their participation in worship through special youth community Masses designed to bring out active participation.

The Individual Dimension

Here are the dialog topics and questions we use:

1. Go Faithfully

At first, Mass seems like a duty to fulfill—an hour we have to give to God. But soon the receiving outweighs the giving. We get strengthened, guided, confronted, or whatever we need. Try comparing a week you went to Mass with a week you skipped Mass and notice the differences.
- What reasons have you found, if any, to go each week?
- What barriers are able to block your weekly worship?

2. Open Up Your Life

Mass is one long, powerful stream of prayer meant to guide and support us as we bring ourselves to God. All through the liturgy, talk to God about what is going on in your life and in your feelings. Listen and watch for words in the liturgy or happenings around you that carry God's response to you. As soon as something hits home with you, respond. Talk right back to what you hear or see and then keep taking in more.
- What parts of the liturgy touch you the most?
- In what ways do you hear or feel God speaking to you during the liturgy?

3. Put Out a Total Effort

People like to talk about the priest and how good his preaching or celebrating is or is not.
- How good a celebrant are you?
- Do you give it all you've got at Mass?
- How much can people get out of a party if they go as spectators?

Make a group list of ways you've found to give of yourself in the liturgy.
- Which items on the list would you like to experiment with more?

4. Meet Christ

Christ comes to the table of meeting with much-needed gifts for all of us, but he cannot deliver them to us unless we also come with the gifts he longs to receive from us. But what could we possibly have that Christ wants and cannot have unless we choose to give it to him? For starters, we can give him our thanks, our apologies, our problems, and our questions. We can also offer him our pain, our love, our decisions, our dreams, and our fears. There is no end to what we can bring to Christ. (Sometimes on retreats we prepare for Mass by writing down and bringing forward during the offertory the gifts we each will offer.)

The Communal Dimension

The key ingredient in training for the communal dimension of a youth liturgy is a priest who is willing to celebrate a special liturgy with the youth at one of their regular gatherings.

Often youth ministers decry the lack of contact between their young people and their all-too-busy priests. But sometimes the real problem is that priests, like most adults, feel a bit awkward around teenagers. We have found an ideal way to bridge not only the generation gap but also the gap between young Catholics and the ones whose primary mission is to lead them into the fullness of worship.

We send an invitation to our priest to celebrate the Eucharist with us. An evening is agreed upon, but no liturgy roles are assigned ahead of time. Everyone just meets in the usual place. After we gather, but before the liturgy starts, everyone chooses a role. Here's the list of roles we use:

- altar arrangers (two people)
- song selectors and leaders (four to eight people)
- lectors (two people)
- composers of prayers of the faithful (four to eight people)
- lay ministers of the Eucharist (two people)
- collection announcer—someone to explain where the collection will go (one person)
- people to pray with the priest for inspiration (two people)
- intercessors—people who pray a decade of the rosary and intersperse it with intentions for a powerful liturgy (the rest of the group members)

Everyone should volunteer for one or more jobs.

All of the jobs entail some preparation, so as soon as everyone has selected a role, the group leader gives a signal and the place suddenly erupts into a beehive of hushed activity. The "hush" is stressed so as to build up, along with the busy involvement, an atmosphere of reverence.

In about ten minutes, everything and everyone is in place, poised for the opening song. The priest (main celebrant) is met with a wave of expectancy and participation that makes worship a light yoke indeed. The priest feels especially cared-about by our invitation. We feel especially cared-about by his coming. The priest is in his element and so are we. Instead of one priest trying to drag everyone else along through the liturgy, we have a mighty team of young horses all yoked with him in one happy effort. When we thus "'are gathered in [Christ's] name'" (Matt. 18:20, RSV), the real presence of Christ, hidden in the bread and the wine, becomes manifest in the voices and faces of his people. We experience ourselves as the Body of Christ.

Our three parish priests take turns being the *main* celebrant. (What kind of party can we have unless all of us see ourselves as celebrants?) These special youth Masses take place every six weeks or so, and I hope our priests won't be embarrassed if I write publicly that they are at their best with the young people. Their preaching is freer—more personal, humorous, challenging. And their praying is freer—more intimate, creative, moving. After such liturgies, I come home ready to shout back at my television screen. For me and all the other TV junkies who were able to tear themselves away for the evening, a new taste for involvement and excitement has been gained. The colorful screen now appears pale and lifeless compared to the reality we have just seen and touched. Now, looking through eucharistic eyes, a devastating word of adolescent denunciation, often misdirected at liturgy, finds its proper mark: Behind all its allurement, *television is boring!*

18
Breakthrough Prayer: Interceding with the Heart

The time was Monday morning, the place was the high school. Cindi was just back from a weekend youth retreat. Her friend, who had declined to attend the retreat, came running up to her. "You prayed for me, didn't you? Come on, admit it. I know you did. I had this sudden peaceful feeling, and I knew it came from you." Cindi's eyes grew wide and her mouth dropped open because, as a matter of fact, she had prayed hard for her friend, using a special kind of prayer we call *intercessory prayer.*

The results are not always this dramatic and quick in the "prayee," but the sense of effectiveness is always there for the "pray-er," even if the good effect is gradual or hidden. Intercession is a distinct and well-defined kind of prayer among Pentecostal Christians, and it was from a tape by one of their finest teachers, Derek Prince, that I learned the technique and adapted it for use with our high schoolers.

Here are the instructions that I give to our young people—usually on the occasion of a retreat:

Pick a person you love and are concerned about, someone you're carrying around in your heart and for whom you feel a burden of worry, someone you would really like Christ to touch. [Then I wait until everyone indicates that they've picked somebody to pray for.]

Now go find a quiet corner, a room, or an outdoor spot where you can pray aloud and not be concerned about anyone giving you weird looks. When you get there, go to work praying for the person you have selected.

Here's how to put spiritual forcefulness into it: Let your prayer be out loud, thorough, inspired, and continuous. I'll explain:

1. Out loud: Put all the urgency you feel into your voice, and tell Christ what's in your heart for this loved one.

2. Thorough: Go into the situation thoroughly, asking for every good thing you feel this person needs. Do not be stingy about details; talk about circumstances, attitudes, other people involved, spiritual barriers, sins, physical problems, and everything else you're aware of. Thoroughly express the good you want to see happen.

3. Inspired: As you pray, new prayer ideas will come to mind. That's the Spirit moving into your work, so let these waves of inspiration direct what you say. Pray everything that comes to you.

4. Continuous: Keep going; push yourself past any temptation to stop until you finally get a distinct sense of relief from the worry that was heavy on your heart. Only stop when you feel you've succeeded in lifting up your loved one to the Lord, when you sense that your loved one's needs are no longer on your shoulders but on Jesus'—where they belong—and when you know you're done because your heart is light and the burden is gone.

The young people return from their intercessory missions in about five or ten minutes, and I make a point of asking what the experience was like for them. Typically they report that the prayer experience was something powerful, something they should use more often. Then we discuss the theology of intercessory prayer a bit. The theology is simply that the young people and Jesus have just done a job of ministry that neither could do alone. The young people needed Jesus, and Jesus needed them. Jesus will not intervene in human affairs unless he is invited. He always waits at the threshold of our need for someone to open the door. To do otherwise would be to violate our freedom of choice. Intercessory prayer is an instance of "'. . . knock, and the door will be opened to you'" (Matt 7:7, NIV). We knock to gain the access, and Christ opens the door and provides the power— not always exactly as we have expected, but because we have asked with all our heart, the Lord's answer can be trusted.

Teens are not the only ones who could stand to use intercessory prayer more often. Fr. Ross Frey, the founder of Teen Encounter at Saint Basil's, says that all face-to-face ministry is only as strong as the intercessory prayer that precedes it. I remember being stunned when he first said that, because too much of what I was passing off as ministry had no prayer at all behind it. My image for ministry now is an iceberg. The relational stuff that goes on is only the visible tip of ministry. The center and momentum of ministry is hidden beneath the surface in the praying we do for people before we actually begin to minister in tangible ways.

I have become convinced that a lot of people burn out and drop out of ministry simply for a lack of enough intercessory prayer. We generously rush to the aid of others but often just end up loaded down with their difficulties. The comfort of our presence and concern is some relief no doubt, but if we go too often without invoking a presence and a comfort beyond our own, our spiritual reserves get depleted. And when that happens, we begin to wonder if we're in the right line of work.

And the job of interceding need not fall only on the shoulders of the individual minister. Backup ministries of intercession can funnel vast amounts of prayer power into the hands of the up-front ministries. Some examples:

- Janet Hesenius, a youth coordinator in Weymouth, Massachusetts, has two friends who get together with her for one hour each week to intercede for their parish teens.
- The professional youth coordinators who meet each month with Fr. Dick Harrington spend their first thirty minutes together in the chapel interceding for the youth of the archdiocese.
- For about six years, our parish youth community has counted on the weekly intercessions of a small group of older parishioners. Toward the end of each youth meeting, the young people put written prayer intentions into our "petition bottle." These petitions are then tucked in an

envelope that is taped to the side door of the church, where one of our faithful intercessors picks it up on the way to Mass the next morning. After Mass, a small group of parishioners opens the envelope and prays each intention one-by-one into the hands of God.

- Paul Cain, one of our adult leaders, has recently made it his business to intercede daily for the youth community and, in particular, for the needs revealed in the petition bottle. One result is that he has suddenly found a new ease in reaching across the generation gap.

My point is that intercessory prayer, itself a ministry, is also the vitalizing source of every other kind of ministry. Of course many, many methods for intercession exist. Fasting, praying the rosary, and celebrating the Eucharist are a few forms of intercessory prayer that people offer with the same kind of all-out involvement and dedication that I have described in the technique we teach.

There is something very active and even physical about the work of intercessory prayer. Two passages that capture the vigorous mood of intercession are Matt. 22:37 and 39: "'You shall love the Lord your God with all your heart, and with all your soul, and with all your mind'" and "'You shall love your neighbor as yourself'" (RSV). Intercessory prayer captures the spirit of both commandments. Both say, "Don't hold back, pray and love with everything you've got." Then prayer is no longer a passive wishfulness but a dynamo that sends out the love in our heart. Teens often worry intensely about their families and friends. They need an outlet to release that worry—and their fierce love—into the intensity of intercession. And so do we all.

19

Dear Jesus: Praying on Paper

For most young people, prayer is simply asking God for things. You can help teens to see rather quickly that any friend who treated them like that really wouldn't be much of a friend. Yes, friends do favors, but a good relationship must develop first. So how do we become friends with God? That's the question that opens up our discussion on prayer.

Saint Francis of Assisi once said that he prayed with only two questions: "Who are you?" and "Who am I?" (See *The Little Flowers of Saint Francis,* by Raphael Brown, Image Book ed. [New York: Doubleday, 1958], 188.) We readily think of prayer as a search for God, but Francis urges us to make it also a search for ourselves. Sometimes prayer can actually become an elaborate escape from self. But Francis helps us to see that we need to stand before God and tell God all we know about who we are. As we express ourselves and sense the love of the Divine Listener, more and more will come out, things we barely knew were there. If we persist, our very souls will finally be revealed and freed to rise up in prayer. We will come away from prayer with a new wholeness, a new sense of self.

This interpretation of Francis's two questions casts prayer as an invitation to open communication between friends, and teens find that idea of prayer quite appealing. The invitation image builds on the prayer forms they've hopefully received at home and in religious education—that is, asking for help, offering thanks, giving praise, and seeking forgiveness. But an invitation to friendship prompts a more free-flowing encounter that involves the young people's own unique emerging senses of self. I often say, "You want to encounter Christ? He will be as real with you as you're willing to be with him."

I will present a technique of prayer based on this relational model of Francis, but first, a word to the would-be instructor. If we enjoy prayer and speak enthusiastically about our own give-and-take with Christ, our teens will be attracted too. A hunger and loneliness for God exists in them, but it's a shy kind of need that only our own openness can touch and bring out. If we candidly entrust to them our own prayer experiences, they will gradually come to trust us as their spiritual mentors and want us to teach them to pray too.

The technique I offer is the "prayer journal." The prayer journal is a way of turning to Christ that I use and love. The teens in our group love it, but yours won't, unless you first experiment with the technique yourself and discover what it can do for you. Then adapt and develop the technique to suit your own spiritual style so that when you give it away, the young people will receive it not as a technique from a book but as a gift from your heart.

The prayer journal is simply praying on paper. It's a letter to God somewhat in the mode of "Dear Diary," except that it begins with "Dear Jesus." I introduce it in the following way:

> Your journal is between you and God. You can be perfectly honest. You will not be asked to share with anyone else what you've written, although you may sometimes choose to. Write as you would to a close, close friend; be yourself. Write whatever comes to mind, and don't stop until you finish the letter. Do not be surprised if your writing goes in unexpected directions. The Spirit will inspire you and guide you. Be open about what you feel as you write; include negative feelings as well as positive ones. Know that a Friend who loves you will instantly receive and welcome each word with the same kind of joy that you feel when a good friend writes to you. Decide how to close your letter—*with love, sincerely,* or maybe something more intense like *very confused,* or *I love you.* Again, write whatever you feel.

We will observe absolute silence among us, so as not to intrude on the space we need to grant one another for our relationship with God. And now here is the first sentence to help you start your letter: "Dear Jesus, . . ."

The first sentence is carefully worded and addressed to Jesus to help everyone get personal with God about whatever concerns they are addressing. Here are examples of letter starters for several different situations:

- To begin a retreat, "Dear Jesus, here's what I hope to gain in coming to this retreat . . ."
- To prepare for reconciliation, "Dear Jesus, please help me to tell you the areas in my life that I need you to forgive and heal."
- To digest a talk, "Dear Jesus, what I hear you telling me in this talk is . . ."
- Or to help a team set goals for an event they will plan, "Dear Jesus, here's what I would like this outing [or other event] to do for the youth community . . ."

Sometimes during journal writing, the promptings of the Spirit become quite apparent. I ask the young people to be ready when that happens to do reverse journal: "Stop writing *to* Jesus and write *from* Jesus. Write whatever you think and feel he's saying to you. Begin, 'Dear Ed . . .' and take it from there."

With an experienced group, I sometimes instruct the young people to go in and out of reverse journal, making the letter a dialog. And on some occasions, I use letter starters that are totally reverse journal. For example: "Dear Ann, what I've been saying to you on this retreat is . . ." Often it takes a while for beginners to warm up to this listening side of prayer, but once they do, their relationship with Christ becomes much stronger. Other ways of hearing Christ, like reading the Scriptures and celebrating liturgy, then take on new meaning as well.

My favorite journal story comes from one of our leadership meetings. I had sent the group off to pray with "Dear [teen's own name], I would like to see the community become stronger in . . ." Kathy, a tenth grader, went to write in her journal with a deeply furrowed brow and came back all smiles. "God really yelled at me," she said enthusiastically. She had been upset and self-righteous over a recent outbreak of cliquishness, but as she wrote, Kathy was shown that some frustrated clique tendencies of her own had been masquerading as unselfish concern for the community. The letter helped

her and others who were listening to remove that particular "beam" from their eyes, and it freed them to deal wisely with the community issue at hand.

Some young people bring the journal technique home and use it for their own prayer times and some don't, but everyone gets some good mileage out of it in the group setting. Praying on paper is easier in the midst of a praying community. And the intense quiet times of journal prayer leave the young people just popping with things to say to one another. A double security exists in having visited their own inner thoughts and in having visited their God. The principle seems to be, If we talk first to God, we have a lot more to offer when we talk to one another—and isn't that the enlivening effect Jesus claimed our friendship with him would accomplish? "'. . . I have come that they may have life, and have it to the full'" (John 10:10, NIV).

20

Oh, I Never Go:
Unlocking the Sacrament of Reconciliation

On one of our youth retreats, Laurie, a sixteen-year-old group member, gave a talk on going to confession. Laurie shared this story:

> I used to worry about what the priest thought of me as I revealed my sins to him, so one time I got brave and asked an older priest if he looks down on people for what they tell him. His answer took me by surprise. He said, "No, just the opposite. I find I really look up to you for your courage to be so honest. And do you know what your confessing does for me? It makes me realize that I need to go to confession too." And he thanked me.

Laurie's story sent ripples of relief through the youth group. We felt one big barrier to reconciliation dissolve. But there are other barriers, major ones. Laurie had made her way past a lot of them, and because she's very peer-credible, her talk was one part of our strategy to reconnect other young people with the forgiving love of Jesus in the sacrament of

111

reconciliation. I'll come back to Laurie's particular journey at the end of the chapter, but first let's look at the general pastoral practice of the sacrament and some strategies that address our problems with it.

The biggest barrier to reconciliation teens face is that so few adults regularly celebrate this sacrament. I once heard a priest from Ireland account for it this way: "We're so busy with the 'I'm okay, you're okay' part of Christianity that we've lost the other part of our identity—of being people who have a great and recurring need to be delivered from our sin. To deny the reality of this need is to deny a part of our very self." But deny it we do, and as a result, I'm told that the quietest hour in a priest's week can be the time he waits to forgive sinners in the reconciliation room.

We forget or ignore confession perhaps because in its revised rite the personal revelation involved is just too scary for many otherwise-devoted Catholics. In its new rite, reconciliation is a journey into ourselves, into the hidden regions of our heart. If this picture of the sacrament is threatening to us as adults, it is bound to be even more so to our young people. Adults and youth need to hear and experience just how freeing this sacrament can be. And we also need to feel the support of the community cheering us on as we do this very individual—and gutsy—thing.

Here are some ways we generate enough encouragement to make this sacrament approachable:

2. We invite a priest to hear confession during one of our regular youth meetings. Then, while he waits in a nearby room, we discuss the sacrament by inviting the group members to reflect and then share an *attitude,* an *experience,* a *belief,* or a *question* regarding the use of this sacrament. During this discussion, anyone is free to slip out of the meeting to the nearby room to celebrate the sacrament with the priest.

3. During Lent, we issue a challenge to make confession one of our Lenten practices in order to get ourselves ready for Easter. The young people then talk in pairs and decide whether to accept the challenge or not and, if so, how to help each other fulfill it—like going to confession together, calling each other afterward, or setting a deadline.

4. Before a major youth event like a retreat, the planning team members will often agree to go to reconciliation as a way of preparing themselves for peer ministry by getting rid of inner obstructions.

5. On a recent twenty-four-hour retreat in the parish center, we laid a length of computer paper on the floor and everyone sat in a circle around it. Then we brainstormed a list of the kinds of sins we felt teens are up against. We scheduled this session at the parish's regular Saturday afternoon reconciliation time. During the easygoing list-building and discussion, people were free to leave and go to the reconciliation room. Several priests were waiting that day. The group joked about how as the list developed people would say, "Oops! I'm outta here." Actually, leaving the discussion group was a little less obvious than that, but that's roughly how it worked.

6. Lastly, nothing can match the power of a young person giving testimony, either in a talk or in an open witness session, about the good things Jesus has done for them through the load-lifting sacrament of reconciliation. In a witness talk on a retreat, Laurie shared her story.

Earlier in the year, Laurie's attitude toward people had started to go sour. The currents of gossip so common in her high school had gotten inside her head, and all she could do was see people's faults. Laurie was troubled because she knew that she was losing her basic liking and appreciation for others. She said she had lost her innocent eyes, and she wanted them back. But the problem was like an infection—growing bigger all the time—and she could not stop it.

Laurie had shared her problem in one of our leadership training sessions and had been advised to avail herself of the sacrament of reconciliation. But she had not done so. Then, a few months later, Laurie joined the retreat team, and the others on the team, remembering the problem she had shared, asked her to do a talk on overcoming spiritual barriers. "But I haven't overcome my problem yet," Laurie responded. "Then do it now for the sake of the people on the retreat," she was told, "and then as a part of your talk, tell what happened." And that's just what Laurie did. She did some journal reflection to get ready for confession and then brought her problem to Jesus in the person of one of our priests. Laurie came out with new eyes. The goodness and beauty of people around her were visible once again. What she had hoped for happened. But the kicker in the story is that Laurie would not have sought out this healing just for her own sake. The incentive of helping others was what she needed to get her moving.

The Gospel passage that best captures Laurie's experience, and maybe even captures the generous motive that would get a lot of us to confession, is Matt. 7:5, "'. . . First take the plank out of your own eye, and then you will see clearly to remove the speck from your brother's eye'" (NIV). The kindest thing we can do for our children, our spouses, and our friends regarding reconciliation is to get our own self to confession. And if I read the passage right, doing this humbling act puts us in the best possible position to be an inspiration and encouragement for others to do likewise. So the *first* strategy (did you wonder where number 1 went?) we adult youth ministers can use to get young people to go to confession is to go ourselves, regularly.

21

Heroic and Hungry: Tapping the Power of Fasting

Mark, a member of our youth group, does a bread-and-water fast every Friday for people and situations that he feels need special help. He knows his fasting would upset his parents, so he fasts without telling them. For that reason, I've used a fictitious name.

Mark says that he sees good results from this method of praying, but the greatest results are some unexpected changes in himself. He's developing willpower, confidence, and self-awareness, all at a rate faster than he can attribute to normal growth and development. He asked me to stress that these benefits seem to come as a surprise, as a bonus, because his intentions when he fasts are focused on others.

Mark's discipline is exceptional, but it didn't develop in a vacuum. Our youth community places great value on fasting, and we fast together on special occasions. In this chapter, I trace the influences and the programs that taught us to trust fasting.

Four strong voices convinced me about fasting, and I passed my convictions along to our young people. These are the four voices:

1. John Wesley, the great founder of the Methodists, who set all of England ablaze with revival at the start of the nineteenth century, only accepted into his ministry preachers who would pray and fast for conversions at least one day a week.

2. John Vianney, the patron saint of priests, was once ordered by a doctor to stop all fasting while recuperating from an illness. The curé obeyed but complained that it cut way back on his soul-rescuing powers in the confessional.

3. Mary, as heard by the teenage visionaries of Medjugorje, Yugoslavia, asks people to do a bread-and-water fast each Friday for peace. She says believers have forgotten what was well-known in biblical times—that fasting can help change the course of both natural and political events.

4. The U.S. bishops, in their peace pastoral, have also called for and committed themselves to serious Friday fasting as a means of waging peace and helping the human family work away from the brink of nuclear war. (See National Catholic News Service, "The Challenge of Peace: God's Promise and Our Response," *Origins* 13 [19 May 1983]: 2.)

These four great authoritative voices all assure us that fasting as a form of prayer can generate a great power for good. But still comes the simple question, likely to be asked by any candid teenager, "How can it possibly help another person if I decide to go hungry?" We Catholics lost that question and its answer when Friday fasting was made into law, and people tended to obey the law. And we have yet to recover for ourselves the persuasive reasons to embrace fasting voluntarily now that the law has been removed.

What good does fasting do? Our youth community holds out four specific benefits:

1. The Physical Effect

Medical personnel assure us that far from being harmful, shutting down the old digestive system for a day every once in a while is a benefit. The hunger pangs do not seem to agree, but once you come to terms with them, you will likely experience a surge of vitality. Digesting food takes a lot of physical energy, and when you stop eating, that energy is released for other uses.

2. The Spiritual Effect

During a fast, prayer goes better. Focusing and expressing yourself is easier, and it's also easier to sense the nearness and the promptings of God. Fasting seems to expand inner space and bring a deeper inner quiet.

3. The Justice Effect

Gandhi is our mentor in the use of fasting for social change. The generosity and commitment evident in a person fasting for justice is a powerful witness to that cause and moves others to commitment as well. Later in this article, I will offer an example.

4. The Ministry Effect

By choosing to bear the discomforts of hunger for the sake of others, we are able to absorb and dissipate some of their troubles. Fasting is a small equivalent of what Christ did for us on the cross. "Ours were the sufferings he was bearing, ours the sorrows he was carrying" is how Isaiah (53:3–4, NJB) describes the process. Fasting is a way we too can "take up the cross."

Most of the fasting in our youth community is done in connection with retreats. For example, retreat planners will often skip a meal or eliminate junk food as an offering for the success of a retreat. Occasionally we offer a retreat based entirely on fasting. The retreat program we use comes from the World Vision organization. They call it "Planned Famine." The program's purpose is to raise both consciousness and funds for world hunger. Young people collect sponsors and fast to raise money for people whose hunger is involuntary. The Planned Famine does a wonderful job of opening up people's hearts and minds to the experience of and the problem of hunger. World Vision provides a kit containing program materials for the thirty-hour retreat. For more information, call their toll-free number, 1-800-444-2522, or write to them at this address:
Attention: Planned Famine
World Vision
919 West Huntington Drive
Monrovia, CA 91016

Recently we have used the same basic approach for other projects like fund-raising for our "adopted" orphanage in Bolivia. And it really is true—people respond generously. During our most recent effort, a gentleman stepped forward and matched the total amount of our sponsors' pledges, which enabled us to send off a very respectable check.

Another big source of encouragement to fast came to us from the Teen Encounter movement. They taught us to do *palanca* (a Spanish word that means "to crank" or "to exert leverage"). *Palanca* can entail any form of a sacrificial act of prayer, but it focuses mainly on some type of fasting. The passage they use is Matt. 17:21, in which Jesus recommends prayer and fasting for the dislodging of certain kinds of evil. Their idea is that fasting for people facing a spiritual challenge, like going on a retreat or writing a talk, works to dislodge their spiritual barriers. One person's effort of fasting backs up another person's effort of spiritual search or ministry. Doing *palanca* has become a foundation stone of our retreats.

We have begun to apply the power of fasting on other occasions. If someone is facing trouble or a major task, a friend will support that person by fasting. To illustrate: at a weekly leadership meeting, one of the newer members of our leadership group was selected to moderate the weekly youth meeting. She admitted that she was both happy and scared. Much to my delight, one person after another piped in with, "I'll fast for you tomorrow." It just happened spontaneously, and I can tell you—quite apart from the invisible effects—that young woman was visibly moved and encouraged on the spot. The meeting she led was one of the best anyone could remember.

And now we come to the big pair of questions: "Should I fast?" and "Should I ask teens to fast?" Well, nowhere in the Gospels does Jesus command us as Christians to fast. He fasts himself, and he gives instructions on fasting, "'When you fast . . .'" (Matt. 6:16, NIV). But Jesus doesn't require fasting as he does so many other actions. He simply says that his disciples will fast (Mark 2:20, NIV). Jesus describes fasting as an almost automatic part of discipleship, and watching our young people explore fasting, I think I can see why he puts it that way. Fasting has a built-in joy; it is not a dark and heavy task at all. Fasting is a challenge that calls forth courage and heroism rarely tapped in teenagers. Also, fasting clearly works. It works powerfully and is a pleasure to exercise. But most of all, when someone we love is struggling and there seems to be no other way to help, fasting is a way to exercise love. Instead of remaining helpless bystanders, we can find in fasting a very practical way to take a strong stand alongside a friend or loved one who needs us.

22

In Times of Trouble: Wielding the Rosary

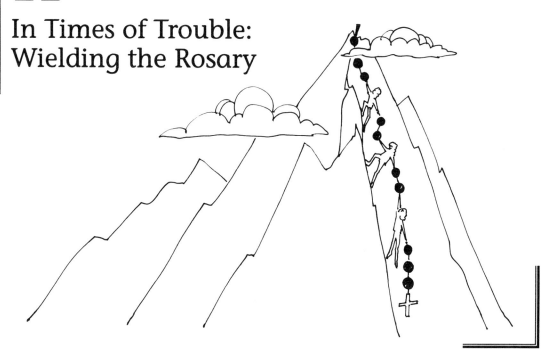

Introducing the Rosary to the Youth Group

When our youth community first took up the rosary, we did so as a way of contending with major trouble—sometimes calling it a spiritual weapon. We accepted Mary's assurance at Fatima that by praying with her in this way, we would wield great power to overcome evil. To equip ourselves with this kind of prayer power, we ran the following announcement in the weekly parish bulletin: "Rosaries needed: If you have any unemployed rosaries gathering dust in your house, the youth community would like to put them to work for you. You can drop them off at the rectory. Thank you!"

The response was immediate. People of the parish poured a deluge of beautiful beads into our laps. The rosaries were cut glass and black wood, pewter and plastic, carved wood and enameled, glow-in-the-dark and colorful, small and large, simple and ornate. The array looked like what it actually was—a sparkling treasure of faith being handed on from one generation to another.

We gave out the rosaries at an overnight retreat, laying them carefully on the carpet, side-by-side like spokes in a great wheel, so that everyone could see them all and could see too the generosity of our elders. Then each young person, with great reverence, selected one to keep, and together we prayed our first rosary. The only instruction was, "Think of someone who you feel has been caught up in the confusion of some evil, and let the sound and meaning of the words we say go to their aid."

At first, a tentativeness prevailed as we prayed. But as one of the adults simply announced each mystery and we prayed in unison, a great sense of quiet gradually encompassed us. By the time we reached the end, no one wanted to stop. Discussing the experience afterward, the young people shared how they had initially expected a boring, mechanical exercise and how they had been surprised at how good it felt to pray this prayer. I had shared the same fear, but time and again I've discovered that ventures like this are ventures in faith. We do our part and trust that God will do likewise. I need not have feared. The rosary proved to be a self-validating experience for the young people.

Praying the rosary is not always a quiet experience. On another overnight retreat we showed a very motivating anti-abortion film called *The Silent Scream*. (The twenty-eight-minute videocassette may be available from your local diocesan office, or contact American Portrait Films, 1695 West Crescent, Suite 500 California Federal Building, Anaheim, CA 92801.) Abortion seemed a big enough evil to warrant taking up our rosaries, so we decided to remain silent after the film, walk directly to the chapel, and express everything we felt through our prayer. The chapel was small and the sound echoed loudly. That rosary became a rising storm of purposeful voices doing invisible but audible battle against the evils of abortion. We went in heavily burdened but came out elated; we had the feeling that somewhere out beyond that chapel, positive benefits were being realized. Maybe someone decided not to abort. And someday, when all things are revealed, we would know who our prayer had helped, but for right then it was enough to sense a power for good going out through us as we prayed.

Private Use of the Rosary

Some years ago I read a little book, *The Secret of the Rosary*, by Saint Louis de Montfort (Rockford, IL: TAN Books and Publishers, May 1981). He said that a rosary before a talk or a homily endows the speaker with a greatly increased power to touch people. I first experienced this effect when I was getting ready to write a retreat talk titled "How's Your Prayer Life?" I decided to pray a rosary first, but it was difficult from the start. I kept getting distracted by interesting ideas for the talk. For a while I fought it, thinking I was being tempted away from the prayer. But finally I realized that this was prayer—the receiving kind. Inspiration kept coming, so I kept stopping to take notes. The rosary took a while, but when I finished, I had a complete outline for my talk. And that talk turned out to be more fun, both for me and for my listeners, than any I had ever done before. Now I would never think of preparing a talk or writing an article without interspersing a decade or two of the rosary between paragraphs.

The rosary is my ministry ace, and I take full advantage of it in another way. Praying a rosary before our weekly youth meeting seems to bring that release of the Spirit I look for in our discussions and interactions during the meeting. The weeks I feel I just do not have time, I notice the difference. Thus, I recommend the rosary as a kind of special strategy for empowering youth ministers.

I suppose the rosary is not going to appeal to everyone, and actually, most days it does not appeal to me either—beforehand. But I do like the results. The rosary is a bit like fasting; it sharpens and focuses attention and increases resolve. And, like everything else we offer to God, the pithy old saying of the Pentecostals applies: "You can't outgive God." All I can say is, try it—you may find you like it.

The Rosary as a Prayer Form

Why does the rosary prove to be so effective? Yes, it's a mystery. But surely the questioning, contemporary part of us deserves more of an answer than that, lest all our bead wielding seem just a pious version of an appeal to magical powers.

From a strictly human standpoint, in the simple act of praying the rosary, several healthy dynamics are at work producing several healthy effects.

The rest effect: During a rosary, everything else stops—work stops, conversation stops, all the onrushing active energies of our personalities have to take a clearly defined break. This short pause in our frantically busy lifestyles is good for the nervous system. We rest. Praying the rosary is stress relief, it's good for the *heart*—and by that word I mean both the blood pump and the feeling self.

The concentration effect: For most of us, our prayer life is constantly prone to distraction from our thought life. The repetitive prayers of the rosary occupy the space of our mental chatter and allow us to sustain the focus of prayer far longer than we would on our own, without such a well-structured format.

The feminine effect: Most of our Catholic imagery is male-oriented. The rosary's attention to Mary helps us to trust this feminine expression of Divine compassion. The masculine and feminine sides of our own spiritualities come into better integration.

The Gospel effect: The fifteen mysteries are an abridged Gospel. Simply to recall each mystery is to re-establish for ourselves the reality of Jesus' impact on our world. We easily lose that reality and slip into a more secular and superficial frame of reference. The rosary refocuses for us what life is really about.

The four effects just described are good ones, no doubt. They may even be persuasive as one is contemplating whether to take up the rosary. But the quieting, centering, balancing, refocusing benefits are still only benefits to the pray-er and do not account for the radical good effects that extend beyond the psyches of the praying individuals to the target of their prayers.

Prayer is a joint effort by the people of earth and the people of heaven—a joint effort that adds to our love a higher love (please see chapter 18). When our hearts and minds are carefully focused in the rosary prayer, we draw near to an amazing woman whose heart and mind are full of extraordinary tenderness and power. Mary is full of grace. The beads in and of themselves have no power. The woman has great power, and united with her, so do we. The secret of rosary effectiveness is as simple and as mysterious as that.

Using the Rosary in the Youth Group

The following are some ways we use the rosary prayer in our youth group:

1. The weekly decade of petitions: Toward the end of our regular youth meeting, we turn off all the lights—except for one candle that remains burning—and the young person moderating picks up the rosary beads and invites us to pray for people we're concerned about. After the Lord's Prayer, the moderator shares the first intention and finishes it by saying,

"Hail Mary . . ." and we all immediately join in. Others add their own intentions before each Hail Mary and then, like the moderator did, gather us all into the intention by saying, "Hail Mary . . ." After ten such prayers, the moderator leads the Glory Be, which signals the end. The prayers are usually for hurting friends, sometimes for family members with problems, and once in a while for events in the news. Occasionally we focus the prayers on the topic area of the meeting—for instance, our school lives, our outreach, our parents.

2. Retreat rosary: We do not usually say a full rosary during a retreat, but on a recent retreat we included a full rosary near the beginning. The leadership team had been of two minds. Some members were wondering if a full rosary would be too much for the new people, who were just joining the group. But we took the leap, deciding to call it a "peace rosary," and we asked five young people to write their own prayers to introduce each decade. The teens wrote beautiful peace prayers for family members, friends in trouble, the youth community, the parish, and the human family. As usual, we ended up feeling glad we had tried it. The retreat proceeded to take off and rise to new heights.

In Mary's current reported appearances in Medjugorje, Yugoslavia, she repeats her call to defeat evil with the rosary, but she adds a bit of advice we have found most helpful. She says we must "pray with our hearts." And that's the way we are exploring the rosary, gradually, as our hearts feel led. We do not push the rosary as a mandatory prayer but reserve it as a prayer that is special, with Mary as special co-pray-er. Consequently, the rosary feels like an adventure each time we pray it. Only a few of our young people pray the rosary with any regularity, although in times of trouble, a lot of them will pick it up. Once, before I was a Catholic, I asked a priest friend, "Why, if we have Jesus, do we need Mary too?" He countered with, "Why does a family need a mother?" And that's how it is for our youth community. We are a family of disciples hearing Jesus say, "'This is your Mother' . . ." (John 19:27, NJB). And so, like Jesus' early followers, our youth community is making a place for Mary in our home.

23

God, I Need You: Training in the Art of Private Prayer

We often challenge the young people in our youth group to develop a daily time for private prayer. Regular prayer is a big challenge, even for adults. Our schedules are too full already. But those who take up the challenge and sustain it even for a short while report great results. Calmness, new perspective, direction—the list is long, the results attractive. Many people wish they could develop a daily prayer time, but they do not quite know how to go about it.

To help people learn how to pray regularly, we developed the *prayer journey*. The prayer journey is a training experience that moves through four personal prayer options first by describing them, then by trying them, and finally by talking about how they went.

Prayer training might sound like the sort of thing teens would least enjoy, but in fact, the prayer journey has been brought back by popular demand again and again—usually on retreats. My guess is that the attractiveness of prayer training lies in the freedom it gives people to be active in prayer, both physically and emotionally. People emerge from the training feeling that prayer is a vigorous, engaging sort of activity, and it leaves them with an appetite for more.

The briefing before the training experience goes like this:

The prayer journey is a journey to God. It won't be an easy journey. You'll have to put everything you've got into it. Four different ways of meeting God are yours to try.

1. The music room: (Songs will be playing.) [Name of young person] has put together a forty-five-minute tape of mostly popular songs, including a few by Christian artists. Many people here can tell you that if you ask God to speak to you about your life, within three songs you will hear something that you will recognize as God's personal message to you. So just go, listen, and be open.

2. Walking the road: Go outside and walk and talk with God. Keep your distance from other people so that you can feel free to say whatever you want. As you walk along, stop talking at intervals and look and listen for whatever might come to you. Maybe God will speak to you through things around you, or thoughts that take shape, or feelings that arise. When that happens, respond and tell God more. Remain honest as you talk and listen, talk and listen.

3. The word room: In the word room you'll find three things: first, some sheets of paper listing a variety of possible feeling states and a scriptural passage to go with each one; second, several copies of a prayer book for young people, called *Tracks;* and third, some Bibles. All of these things are there for you to rummage around in while you are asking God to speak to you personally. Search until you find the words that get right at your need. Look for a reflection on one of the sheets that captures how you're feeling, and then look up the scriptural passage given with it. Or, open a Bible or a copy of *Tracks* and read whatever catches your eye.

4. The praise room: The praise room is the most strenuous room and often the most powerful. In this room, you sit in a circle with others and tell God out loud anything positive you feel—things you're grateful for, things you love God for, things you find amazing and inspiring, things you're feeling right at the moment. The challenge that goes with this room is to keep the praise going. When one person finishes praising God, someone else should try to pick up the prayer and keep it going.

You'll find the current of prayer just keeps getting deeper and stronger the longer it continues.

Those are the four areas. Now here are the ground rules:

a. Follow the urge of the moment in deciding where to go and how long to stay. Let the Spirit lead you.

b. Be totally honest with God. If you are not real with God, how is God going to be real with you? Say just what you feel—laugh, weep, be angry, be confused, but be yourself.

c. Stay clear of any social interaction. Do not interfere with what God and you, or God and your friend, are trying to develop.

d. Your goal is to break through with God. That's God's goal too, but you are allowed to set the pace. So push yourself a little. Be aggressive. The harder you seek, the more you'll find.

After you have gone over the ground rules, you can tell the young people to begin their prayer journey. You may need to issue the reminder not to talk again, discreetly, to individuals who find silence difficult.

One adult who is comfortable with praise should stay with the praise room the whole time to help that prayer happen, because praise is the most challenging of the prayer modes. Otherwise, the adults should go on the prayer journey along with the teens.

After about forty-five minutes, people should regather and share how the journey went for them. Take about fifteen minutes to allow people to tell their stories, their adventures with God. Also, include a question such as "Did anyone run into difficulty?" Some people may be dealing with barriers and may need help with them.

The final sharing question should be "Which prayer mode do you want to take home with you and use on your own?" With a group of more than fifteen people, you can pose that question by asking, "How many people want to use *praise* again after the retreat? *walking and talking? the word room? the music room?"* The simple act of answering yes to any of the prayer forms plants the seeds for future good experiences with prayer.

Once the prayer journey experience is over, especially if it has taken place during a retreat, each participant faces a personal decision: Will I now make the effort to build my own private prayer life? The support of the weekly youth meeting will contribute to sustaining a decision to do so. So also will some practical tips we developed that teens can use at home to develop their repertoire of prayer styles. These tips incorporate some of the techniques introduced on the prayer journey and add a few others. You can find the practical tips in the next section of this chapter. (Instead of orally passing on these ideas, you might consider typing them up in handout form and passing them out to retreat participants.)

Along with offering the prayer journey training experience, the weekly youth meetings, and the prayer tips, the final thing we do in support of the budding prayer lives of our young is to go to our own secret places and pray for the courage, the desire, and the persistence the young people will need in order to keep prayer as the wellspring of their life.

The Gospel passage that urges us to build up a rich repertoire of private prayer styles is Matt. 6:6, "'But when you pray, go to your private room, shut yourself in, and so pray to your Father who is in that secret place, and your Father who sees all that is done in secret will reward you'" (NJB). The purpose of the prayer journey is to build up in young people a keen sense of just how rewarding it can be to go off by themselves and seek the presence of their God.

Practical Tips for Prayer

Prayer in the Thick of Things

"'Behold, I stand at the door and knock; if any one . . . opens the door, I will come in. . . .'" (Rev. 3:20, RSV)

Goal
The goal of prayer in the thick of things is to let Christ be your friend and help you in moments of need, which he wants to do but only can do if you ask him.

Practical Tips
- When a stressful situation catches you by surprise, do *instant prayer,* such as "Help me, Lord" or "Sorry, God"—out loud if no one is nearby.
- When you're involved with others and need inspiration for the right words or actions, do *sneaky prayer,* which is praying inside yourself while keeping a straight face outside.
- Before a major challenge—such as an exam, an athletic event, or an important phone call—do *step-aside prayer,*

which can be a brief walk, a visit to a bathroom stall, or just a long stare at the ceiling.

- When help, guidance, or strength is given in response to your asking, do not treat it as a coincidence. Give back some *thanking prayer,* using any of the prayer methods given here.

Real-life Example
Jason used to panic and blank out during tests. Even when he had studied thoroughly, he did poorly. Then he started praying for calmness. He got it, and immediately his grades shot up.

Prayer at Mass

> . . . He was known to them in the breaking of the bread. (Luke 24:35, RSV)

Goal
The goal of prayer at Mass is to come away from Mass with a secure feeling that you've connected with God in a real way.

Practical Tips
- When you arrive for Mass, kneel down and speak to God as personally as you would speak to a friend. You could say something such as *I've missed you, I'm hurting, I'm sorry, I need your help,* or just *Hello!*
- Early in the Mass, tell God what is on your mind. Be honest. Tell God everything that you are feeling. God already knows your thoughts and feelings, but if you do not share them, things are not out in the open between you. God will be as real with you as you are with God.
- Listen to everything that is said and watch everything that happens during Mass, and you will hear God talking back to you about your life.
- When you go up for communion, open up your very self, and Christ will come to you with peace, courage, healing, understanding—or whatever else you may need.

Real-life Example
Melissa used to question whether the Eucharist really was Christ. Once on a retreat, she was sitting on the floor looking at the consecrated host exposed on the altar for prayer, and she became upset over it and voiced all her doubts. A sudden peace came over her that left her permanently convinced of Christ's real presence in the Eucharist.

Prayer with Music

"Today, when you hear his voice,
do not harden your hearts . . ." (Heb. 3:15, RSV)

Goal

The purpose of prayer with music is to hear God speak a personal message to you through popular music. Because popular music is the language of teenage feelings, God will use this language with those who listen.

Practical Tips

- When you decide to listen for something from God, take all love songs as applying to your relationship with Christ and with friends.
- Whenever you turn on the radio, tell Christ you're listening for anything he wants to tell you. Father Don Kimball, the priest-DJ who originated this prayer method, says that within three songs you'll hear something that you know is meant for you.
- If the song promotes something immoral, listen to the Spirit within you encouraging you to take your own stand against the harmful message.
- Especially in your really up times and in your really down times, listen to the music for words that help you celebrate and give thanks, or words that help you feel comfort and hope.

Real-life Example

Anne Marie was told by an adult she confided in to lower her hopes about colleges she wanted to get into. She felt totally put down. Then she heard "Spotlight," by Madonna, and through the song God restored her self-confidence.

Prayer in Times of Quiet

"But when you pray, go into your room and shut the door . . ." (Matt. 6:6, RSV)

Goal

The goal of prayer in quiet times is to set aside special moments to be alone with Christ and to open up your concerns in order to renew and develop your personal relationship with him.

Practical Tips

- *Dialog:* When your heart is full of strong feelings, you need to pour them all out in prayer, and Christ is only too glad to listen. He answers in many ways—sometimes peace or insight will come immediately, sometimes it will come later through someone else or something that happens. But Christ always responds, and things change. Most often it's your attitude that is changed for the better.

- *Journal:* Sit down and write Jesus a heart-to-heart letter. As you put your feelings into words, new ideas will come to you. Write whatever you feel, the Spirit will help you. The letter will develop in ways you do not expect. Keep writing nonstop until you feel you're done.
- *Scripture:* Some people can open the Bible anywhere, and God will speak to them personally through whatever they find. Others like to use the monthly calendar of daily readings, or simply explore. Start by asking Christ to speak to whatever is going on in your life. Then read and underline with a pencil the passages that speak to you. Then talk to the Lord about these passages.
- *Rosary:* When someone you care about is in trouble, take up the rosary and use it as a weapon for defeating evil. You'll be praying *with,* not *to,* Mary. Her prayers have special power to overcome Satan. As you pray each bead, think about what you're asking God to do.

Real-life Example
Kathy saw other people's talents emerging but saw none in herself. Then she read 1 Cor. 12:1–11 and realized that God gives gifts to everyone. Through the verses Kathy read, she was given the confidence to believe that her gifts would emerge, and they did.

24

It's No Coincidence:
Hearing God In Chance Happenings

Jean-Pierre de Caussade, the great Jesuit mystic and author of *Abandonment to Divine Providence,* wrote "[God] speaks to every individual through what happens to them moment by moment. Instead of hearing the voice of God in all these things, . . . men see in them only material happenings, the effects of chance or purely human activities" (Image Book ed. [New York: Doubleday, 1975], p. 43).

A special degree of faith is needed to find the hand of God in chance occurrences, especially painful ones. But the great mystics seem to agree that nothing is left to chance, for God is sovereign. God always brings good out of evil and life out of death—however disguised the hand of God may be. In this chapter, I present four techniques that cultivate faith in the grace of God as it comes through the "random" happenings in our life. In all four of these techniques, people receive—by random selection—something or someone we ask them to work with and regard as an opportunity for being touched and gifted by God.

1. **Tracks:** *Tracks* is an exquisite little book of prayers and photos published and distributed free by the Sacred Heart League. (Copies of the book can be ordered from Apostolate of the Printed Word, Sacred Heart League, Walls, MS 38686; phone: 601-781-1360.) The language is adolescent, the meaning profoundly adult, the tone never condescending. We invite our teens to pause, to think about what's going on in their life that could use prayer, and then to open that book randomly. We ask the young people to read any prayer they come to and to listen for the voice of God speaking personally to their situation—maybe through the whole prayer, maybe in one sentence or phrase, maybe even in just one word. "You'll know when you read the message that it is meant for you because of the way it will hit home," we tell them. After the young people finish listening to God, we invite them to share the messages that came through to them. The coincidences of relevant messages are quite wonderful.

2. **Retreat partners:** On retreats, we often pair up the young people randomly and then send them off to discuss a scriptural passage, a teen issue, or a talk they have just heard. We form the pairs by writing everyone's name on a card and then dividing the cards into two equal piles—one of more experienced and one of less experienced retreatants. A designated moderator shuffles both piles and then picks a name from the novice pile. The person whose name has been selected then picks a partner by choosing a card from the veteran pile. This selection process is repeated until everyone has a partner. Then the randomly selected pairs go off to discuss the topic at hand, listening for what God may want to say to them through what they say to each other.

3. **Messages:** The message technique can be done with any kind of inspired written material. Some of our youth group members and I visited Medjugorje, Yugoslavia, and were convinced of the genuineness of the apparitions of Mary occurring there. Since then we sometimes include Medjugorje in our group activities. If your group is similarly interested in the apparitions, you may enjoy this technique. Take a sheet of the monthly messages revealed by Our Lady to the young persons to whom she appeared in Medjugorje and cut it into individual messages. We pray a decade of the rosary and then each person randomly chooses a message. Everyone then shares how the message they received speaks to their life. The same activity works quite well with a batch of people's favorite biblical passages.

4. Prayer partners: In this technique, everyone writes and signs their name to a prayer that expresses their most urgent concern. These prayers are then shuffled and handed out, one to each of us. We go home and for that week back up with our own prayers the person assigned to us by the random selection.

In each of the four techniques, the moment of random selection is preceded by a simple faith statement like this:

> We believe that God is acting in all the happenings in our lives, even the chance happenings. That means the person whose name we draw (or the passage, prayer, or intention) is a gift from God. What God is offering through this gift may be quite clear, or we may have to work with it awhile to unwrap what God really intends for us to receive.

This is a bold statement of faith, and it is also a challenge to surrender and open ourselves and our immediate futures to the good graces and the will of God.

Some people like to use the Bible itself as a way of hearing from God, randomly opening it and listening to whatever comes through the words they read. Once at the end of a class session, one of our CCD teachers told her class of fourth graders about this method. But one lad was openly skeptical. "Go ahead and try it," said the brave teacher. When he did, he came up with Matt. 9:6, "'. . . Take your mat and go home'" (NIV). That class went home laughing but also marveling.

Some adults (but few teens) bridle at the practice of random selection as a way of listening for God's voice. The practice pushes most of us to a theology of more immediacy and simplicity than our spiritualities easily tolerate. Something in me tries to object too, but I silence that voice on three grounds. First, the material we choose to work with is always good, so even if this randomness thing is just foolishness, we cannot go very far off track with it. Second, it's fun. The suspense and the Christmas-morning-like delight as people unwrap God's grace make for some happy moments. Third, it works. Often enough, the message that comes through is stunningly helpful.

Do the Scriptures anywhere support random happenings as moments of revelation? Saint Paul, in that often-quoted passage from Rom. 8:28 writes, "We know that in everything God works for good with those who love him, who are called according to his purpose" (RSV). Hopefully, through trusting and finding God in our contrived little exercises of randomness, we will go out into the vast seeming randomness of everything that life deals out to us and find there also the guiding and blessing—and challenging—hand of Jesus.

25

A Likable Lent:
Planning Lent for Personal Growth

At age fifteen, Artie was a fairly rambunctious young man. On the one hand, he was full of enthusiasm for the youth community and for Christ. On the other hand, he spoke whenever he got the urge, regardless of who else was speaking, and it was sometimes hard to get him to walk around youth-room furniture instead of over it. Let's just say self-discipline was not his greatest asset at that moment in his development.

So it was a surprise when Artie said to me one April, "Bob, guess what I got for Lent! I passed French, and all my other grades are up, too!" (He only spoke in exclamation points.)

"Was that what you asked for? Was that the heart goal you sent out?"

"Yes, and you know how it happened! I started doing homework! You wouldn't believe how much homework I do now!"

The satisfaction written all over Artie's face spoke of some sort of personal victory over darkness, a resurrection from academic death.

Behind Artie's story is the story our whole youth community lived out that Lent. Most years, Lent caught us off guard, and we would improvise a few last-minute advisories like "Lent is a time to deepen your prayer life" or "Lent is a time to uproot your selfishness" or "The sacrament of reconciliation is a good way to get ready for Easter . . . and so is donating to hunger relief." Good advice surely, but it was not all that effective. We did not have a real Lenten plan.

Then came a February when our leadership group did some concentrated listening prayer with reverse journals (see chapter 19), and here's the full-blown strategy we put together for the first effective Lent the youth community ever had:

1. We decided to treat Lent like a six-week retreat, retreats being the most powerful times of spiritual breakthrough we knew. Unlike most retreats, which step back from the rough challenges of daily life, this retreat would be conducted "on location," right in the midst of normal life situations that often intimidate and defeat us.

2. We unveiled our Lenten retreat plan at the Sunday youth meeting prior to Ash Wednesday with a dramatic dialog (see "I Don't Do Lent" at the end of the chapter). The dialog presents Lent as a time to name the toughest challenges we face in our daily life, to set goals for heart changes that allow us to master these challenges, and to pick a daily action prayer to back up not only our *own* heart goals but one another's.

3. We each formulated our own personal Lenten plans by writing down our main challenges, our heart goals, and our chosen daily action prayer. We put these in a letter to the group of older parishioners who pray for us every week (see chapter 18). And one thoughtful young man suggested that we ask that group of parishioners to send us their Lenten heart goals as well, so that both groups could pray for each other during Lent. They gladly sent us a fat envelope of their heartfelt intentions, and at the rest of the Lenten Sunday evening youth meetings, one young person after another prayed aloud for the intentions of our elder counterparts.

4. We approached each Sunday meeting during Lent as a time to support one another in our Lenten commitments. And each meeting's topic focused on transforming the heart. The topics were integrity, temptations, problem solving, service, and prayer life.

As we came into Holy Week, a kind of crescendo could be felt among us, not all of it pleasant, but all of it rich with the very real struggle for better lives. One young man who had fallen into a pattern of mistreating other members was asked (by me) to take a "leave" until he sorted out and rooted out his abusive behavior. And he opted to stay away for several months. One unhealthy love relationship finally broke up with much agony and distress but also with much relief and a sense of new life when it was over. One young woman who had lost her boyfriend in an accident the previous summer finally came to peace about his death. And Artie got his grades up.

The general trend over the Lenten period was an experience of being able to live out our faith in God in the real events of our life. Challenges that might have been too big otherwise were met and dealt with.

I would characterize this experience of Lent as a kind of cleansing fire that even when it was painful, left everyone with brighter faces and freer hearts. And I'm sure this is at least part of what Jesus wanted for us when he said, "'I have come to bring fire to the earth, and how I wish it were blazing already'" (Luke 12:49, NJB).

Lent Skit: "I Don't Do Lent"

The following is a skit that we have used to help the group see Lent as an opportunity for service and self-growth:

A: I don't like Lent at all. It's just a time the church asks us to be hard on ourselves, and I say life's hard enough already. What am I giving up for Lent? Here's my answer—nothing!

B: Good answer. You have no business doing Lent because you obviously have no idea what it's about.

A: All right Mr. [Ms.] Smart Catholic, we can play hardball. Why don't you tell me—what's so great about Lent?

B: Okay, you asked. I'll give it to you straight. Lent is a time to be very, very good to yourself. What do you think about that? It's just the opposite of what you think, isn't it?

A: You're serious, aren't you? And I can see if I give you half a chance, you're gonna try to sell me on Lent. All right, go ahead. Take your best shot. But you better realize you've got two strikes against you. Number one, I've been there. I grew up in it, and I know Lent is no fun. Number two, your opening line about being good to yourself sounds really ridiculous.

B: Sure it does, to most people, but not if you look at what Jesus really was doing when he went off alone for forty days and did the first Lent.

A: I know what he did—he fasted and he was tempted by the Devil. Sounds like a swell time, doesn't it?

B: The best. Let me show you. Can I ask you three fairly personal questions?

A: Be my guest.

B: Don't give me any details, but just tell me—did you ever get hurt bad by someone, bad enough so that whenever you think of that person, you get really upset?

A: Actually, yes.

B: Do you ever do things at home that just cause trouble for the people you care about and for yourself too?

A: Do I have to answer that? All right, yes!

B: Do you ever wish you could do something or say something, and it's really important to you, but when the time comes you lose your nerve?

A: Hey, wait a minute. Have you been reading my diary or what? How do you know all that about me?

B: Because you're a human being, and you have a human heart with hurts and sins and blockages just like the rest of us.

A: Whoa, you got me there. Behind the masks we put up, everybody's heart sometimes gets broken and selfish and stuck shut. I knew that.

B: Right, but look, what if I could hand you something that would give you the power to throw off all these things that defeat your heart and rob your happiness?

A: I'd take it, right now!

B: Okay, I give you Lent!

A: What? You're kidding, aren't you? Uh oh, I've got a funny feeling you're going to have me wanting to do Lent in a minute.

B: Don't you see? Lent is a fight to stick up for your own heart the way Jesus did. He showed us how not to get knocked down and buried the way you and I do. He took forty days and faced the same heart-crushing forces we face, except he beat them.

A: Oh boy, you mean temptations, don't you? Jesus fought his, and I don't fight mine. I pretty much just go along with all the self-centered ideas that come along. And look where it gets me—cold on the outside and sad on the inside. I've got a lump of lead where my heart should be. God, I've been stupid. It makes me so mad to think about it.

B: Mad enough to fight back?

A: Okay, you win. I'll fight. I'll do Lent. So what's the plan of attack?

B: Hey, now you're talking. This is good stuff. You won't regret it. Here's how it works. Step one—you start the way Jesus did by setting some personal heart goals. He was getting ready for a challenging ministry, and he wanted to clear his heart of anything that would sidetrack him or get in the way of his love. That was his heart goal, and he set aside forty days for it.

A: Hold on, that was Jesus. Are you sure that really applies to me?

B: Well, doesn't your life present you with some tough challenges too?

A: Tough? No, not tough. Impossible, yes, that's the word.

B: Fine, so take a look at your situation and see what your heart needs so you can take these challenges in stride. Lent says, set up your goals like Jesus did—heart goals. And set 'em high. Believe in what you can be and go for it. That's step one.

A: Okay, I'm rolling. How's this? I want to drop some old grudges and feel good inside again. I want to have room for other people, especially one certain person at home. And I want to be free to give what I've got, especially at work [school]. I hope I'm not asking too much, but this is what I want, and I want it a lot or I know I won't really be happy, at least not inside where it counts. This is like a Christmas list, isn't it?

B: No. It's better. It's a Lent list. It's not a list of things you want, it's a list of things you want to be. And by the way, I think you came up with a great Lent list.

A: Thanks, Coach. I've got my heart goals—I know where I need to go. But now I need step two; how do I get there?

B: You have to do something drastically good. It has to be something tangible, something you can do every day that tells God and yourself that you're not just talking with these heart goals of yours—you mean business. Step two is coming up with your own daily Lenten action prayer.

A: Like giving up candy?

B: Maybe, but it doesn't have to be giving up something. It might be starting something—like a prayer journal or a daily walk or taking your wife out regularly or a daily Mass or giving special time to each of your kids or a daily rosary for people you love.

A: Hey, I thought I was supposed to be hard on myself!

B: I told you that you had it all wrong. Your Lenten action prayer should be something you feel good about and kind of wish you were already doing, something really good for you. But don't decide too fast (excuse my pun). Be like Jesus. The Gospels say, "He was led by the Spirit into the wilderness." Ask God to lead you to the perfect action prayer for you, and then look for the one that really clicks.

A: Okay, so in step two I pick an action prayer, or God does.

B: Right.

A: And doing this action will achieve the heart goals on my Lent list?

B: Wrong. Heart goals aren't like that. We have to want these changes, and name them, like you did. But nothing we do will actually accomplish them. The troubles and the hopes of our heart are just too big for our little efforts and abilities.

A: Then *why* are we doing these action prayers?

B: The action prayers are just a way of reaching out to God by doing the kinds of things he asks us to do. They are a way to say, "Here I am, God. I'm serious about us. I'm with you." The action prayers bring us close enough to God for step three.

A: Another step! But what else can I do?

B: Nothing. Step three is what God does. If your heart has dared to aim for wholeness, and if your hands have dared to act with love, then you've prayed the biggest prayer you can pray. You've opened up the door only you can open—the door to God. And now God can act. Actually, it's Jesus. He comes into your Lent and goes to work right alongside you.

A: I get it—step three is all the things that will happen to me during Lent. And I have no control over them, except to let them in.

B: Yes, and you know what? I can't say this for sure because it's all up to God, but I'm going to predict, from listening to you now, that you're going to have a great Lent.

A: Okay, so now you're a prophet. Do you mind giving me a clue about this glowing future you see before me?

B: Mind? You don't know how much I'm enjoying this. I predict you're going to start getting a lot more out of Mass. And reconciliation will be very powerful for you. Don't miss that! And Holy Week especially is gonna knock your socks off.

A: Sounds good to me.

B: Yup, and I predict your little list of heart goals is going to be small compared to what Jesus will do for you and in you.

A: Hey, you know what, you're some kind of salesperson. I love Lent already, and I'm barely into it. It's like an old friend of mine once said, "Lent is a way to be very, very good to yourself."

26
Open Your Mind's Eye: Meeting Christ Through Visualizations

With her blossoming social confidence, Kim was in rare form at school that day. Feigning friendliness to Linda, Kim led the insecure girl on with fake compliments and poisonous sweetness. The onlookers were dying with half-concealed laughter, and Linda was left bewildered.

That evening on the phone, Kim relayed her exploits to Delia, a fellow youth group member, who responded, "Kim, I don't believe you did that." Delia put Kim on hold to take another call. During that pause, Kim saw a mental picture of Linda and Jesus looking at her—Linda kneeling with a hurt and wondering expression, Jesus standing with an angry expression in which Kim read, "How could you do this? She belongs to me too, you know."

Stunned, Kim got off the phone as quickly as she could and burst into tears of remorse. She later told the story at a youth meeting, ending it with, "And now I think Linda and I are going to become real friends. Her affection matters more to me than the phony friendships of the more popular kids."

The mental picture that aroused Kim's conscience so powerfully came suddenly, but her ability to imagine Jesus in this way came neither suddenly nor surprisingly. She had developed it through a technique called visualization, which we often employ in our youth meetings. Visualization, a guided experience of prayer, calls upon and cultivates the imagination. Virtually every group member learns to visualize as a way to contact Jesus. And once in a while, as in Kim's story, the imagination works as a way for Jesus to contact them.

"Having visions" can seem a bit off the deep end, so before I explain how we go about it, I had best build a little credibility. The technique, often called guided meditation, is used by many youth ministry professionals in our diocese, especially on retreats. Each of us adapts it according to our own personal spirituality and pastoral style, and all of us are impressed with the benefits it brings.

The technique of visualization has some respectable roots. The spiritual exercises of Saint Ignatius entail visualizing a scene from the Scriptures and then interacting with Jesus and others in the scene. The charismatic movement has contributed a "healing of memories" technique that entails letting Jesus go with you into painful scenes from the past and watching him say or do things to heal the wounds or their lingering effects. And the Benedictine spirituality that's flourishing in Pecos, New Mexico, teaches a technique called "active imagination," which allows dialog with elements of one's personality—possibly dream figures, one's pain, or one's suppressed feelings.

The first visualization I tried with our youth group came from a retreat that one of our members had participated in. I instructed the group members to close their eyes and imagine themselves on a sandy beach. Then I told them to notice the blue sky and the puffy clouds. I encouraged them to feel the sand under their feet and the warmth of the sun on their backs. I continued by giving the following instructions (with suitable pauses between sentences):

> Now you are walking along the edge of the water, letting the waves occasionally wash over your ankles. You come to a huge rock formation, and you have to wade out a little way into the water to get around it. Then you notice a cave entrance high in the rock. You climb up the rock formation and crawl through the cave's opening. The thrill of adventure fills you as you crawl through the dark passage toward a light. Finally you come to a tiny chapel

hewn out of the rock. The chapel is lit by sunlight coming through a rock crystal ceiling. You sit down on a small stone bench and suddenly notice on the altar a small compartment with a closed curtain. You feel drawn to the compartment. You pull back the curtain and take out a small scroll. You unroll the scroll and find a beautifully lettered message from God. Read what it says.

Then I led the group members out of the chapel, back to the beach, and from there back to the present.

Whenever our group does that visualization, much excitement and enjoyment surface as people share—if they choose to—their messages. One time, a young man who previously had never thought of becoming a religious reported reading the word *priest*. He told us, "I bolted out of the chapel and cave so fast . . ." Now, ten years later, he is considering the priesthood as one of his life options.

Another simple visualization our group has enjoyed for years involves looking at a statue or a picture of Jesus. The only instruction is this: "Think for a minute about whatever is uppermost in your heart, the main concern you're feeling at this moment. Now look at the face of Jesus, especially his eyes, and see what his expression is telling you." Then all the group members look in silence at the statue or picture for about thirty seconds, after which people who choose to share what Jesus told them can do so. One candid young man once told us that Jesus looked very stern to him, and he realized that the look was about some books he had taken from the publishing warehouse where he worked. "I think I had better put the books back," he concluded.

In our group, the most effective visualizations have proved to be the active imagination, eyes-closed encounters with Jesus. So we have gradually come to specialize in that type.

Most often we use the visualization technique in group settings, but occasionally I have helped individuals in counseling sessions to see and hear Jesus through visualization. For instance: Joe, a young man in his senior year, found himself stalled and blocked partway through his Eagle Scout project. He guessed that his mind-block had to do with several experiences of getting beaten up when he was younger and undergoing a residual loss of confidence. Through visualization, Joe went back with Jesus to those painful events, and Jesus simply said things that set him free of a lingering sense of humiliation. Joe suddenly became a dynamo of ambition and brought the Eagle Scout project to magnificent completion.

Joe was at home with the visualization technique because he had used it with us in group meetings. At the end of this chapter, I have included a variety of favorite group visualizations and a list of twelve how-tos that I have arrived at over the years and now use every time I lead a visualization.

A word of caution for anyone who does one-to-one visualization, or any kind of private counseling with teens: Most of us are not trained counselors, and such meetings place us in a position of legal risk. Beyond one session, parental consent is necessary. The young people may not want you to contact their parents, but you can explain that even school counselors are required by law to do the same thing. And you can assure them that confidentiality will still be respected.

Questions about the visualization technique do arise. What about the young person who says, "I just couldn't do it; I didn't see anything"? We say in response, "Be patient. Keep at it. Sometimes it takes a few tries to activate your imagination in this way." In fact, it usually does take only a few tries to learn.

What about a message that seems contrary to the Gospel? We look carefully, and if that's the case, we throw the message out. Everything we think we hear in prayer must always meet the Gospel standard.

What about a disturbing message—like a young man who got an empty box when invited to receive "the gift he was being asked to give the community"? Actually, he had been using and conning the group, so we just asked him to think about what that empty box might mean.

What is the actual source of what we see and hear? Is it really Jesus? Or is it just an expression of one's own best thoughts? I would say both. In John 14:26, Jesus says, "'But the Counselor, the Holy Spirit, . . . will . . . bring to your remembrance all that I have said to you'" (RSV). I'm convinced that in these visualizations the Holy Spirit gathers up all we've come to believe about Jesus and adds an unmistakable sense of love to bring him alive with the right word of wisdom to feed the soul's current need. In the sharing we always do after a visualization, the atmosphere is typically electric with delight at the good things, the freeing things, people bring back with them. Visualizations are fun to lead, fun to experience, and fun to talk about, and I mean the deep kind of fun that the Bible calls *joy*. So my advice is to give visualizations a try, and enjoy!

Visualization Themes

A caution: All of the themes described in this chapter are far too condensed for actual use in leading a visualization. You will need to elaborate the themes with details and directions. I have found that trying out a theme privately brings to mind many of the details and directions you can use for leading the visualization.

1. You are on a walk in the country. You see two paths into the woods. You pick the "one less traveled by." The path gets steep at one point. At another point it comes to a small clearing. On a table in the clearing, you see a wrapped gift. Jesus explains that this is something you need for your spiritual journey. You open the gift and ask Jesus about it. He explains. (Contributed by Sr. Margaret Griffiths)

2. Picture yourself at the border between this world and the next. You have traveled there on a mission of mercy for a loved one. Jesus meets you and places on your shoulder a small bag containing balls of light, each about the size of a snowball. When you take a ball out and toss it up and catch it, it automatically doubles in size. These balls of light are pure healing power. Juggle one enough to make it the size you feel it needs to be to encompass your loved one and his or her problem, and then send it off. See your target person begin to shine as healing and happiness settle upon him or her. (Contributed by Greg Zlevor, who found it in *A Book of Games: A Course in Spiritual Play,* by Hugh Prather [New York: Doubleday, 1981], p. 97)

3. You go to your front door and look out at your yard and neighborhood. You see Jesus walking up to your door. How is he dressed? You walk beside him and talk with him about a challenge you are facing in your life. As you near the church, he disappears, but you sense him drawing you on. You enter and kneel before the tabernacle. Suddenly Jesus is there, appearing in glory. You ask him about a challenge you feel the youth group is facing. He speaks.

4. You go to the place that you reserve for private prayer and begin to tell Jesus how you feel about your prayer life. You ask him what he would like you to do to open up more fully. You talk about his suggestions. Eventually, Jesus gives you a single word to take with you and use to guide yourself the next time you come to him in prayer.

Visualization How-tos

How to Prepare for a Visualization

1. Plan out the whole visualization ahead of time and outline it on paper. Even though visualizing is very personal, the experience depends on someone to guide it—except of course when it comes unexpectedly, as in Kim's story from the beginning of this chapter.

2. In planning and outlining a visualization, prepare instructions that balance. In other words, the instructions for each step should be direct but also open-ended. For example: "Jesus comes up to you. How do you greet each other?" Or, "You ask Jesus about your love life. What is it that you most need help with?"

3. Before giving any instructions, offer a short prayer invoking the presence and guidance of Christ, just as you would at any other kind of youth meeting. Including Jesus at the outset is important. Then the experiences people have are recognized as a part of Jesus' broader work with them, not just as odd, isolated experiences having only a curiosity value.

4. Turn off the lights in the youth room and tell everyone to find a comfortable *sitting* position. (People who lie flat will often doze off, and their heavy breathing or snoring can become a distraction to the group.) As the leader, you can hold a candle to enable you to follow the outline.

5. Direct the participants to close their eyes and relax. Several relaxation techniques can be used. From the Lamaze natural childbirth people comes the *cleansing breath*—a deep intake of air followed by a long slow exhale. The cleansing breath is repeated three times.

Or from the stress management people comes the *muscle tension and relaxation method*—an energetic tightening of body areas and then a complete releasing of those muscles, including the feet, calves, thighs, pelvis, abdomen, shoulders, arms, fists, neck, and face.

Or give simpler instructions like these: "Let yourself feel the peace of Christ all around you. Relax into your chair [or the floor]. Let it support you totally. Now notice any tension anywhere in your body and dissolve it into the feeling of comfort and peace."

How to Guide a Visualization

6. Instruct the participants to go, in their mind, to their favorite place to be alone. The place can be a vacation spot, one's own room, or any other location that is appropriate to the particular theme of the visualization. Tell the group members to notice the particulars of their immediate surroundings, for example, the time of day, the season, the weather, the sounds, and the colors.

7. Ask the participants to visualize Jesus coming toward them in this place. Ask them to watch him coming and notice first how he is dressed—contemporary or Galilean—and then ask them, "What mood or feeling is Jesus expressing to you through his eyes?" Also ask, "What sort of greeting do you give each other—maybe a hug, a word, or a touch?" All these details later prove to have significance.

8. Instruct the group members to tell Jesus about some issue in their life. The issue could involve relationships at home, maybe their prayer life, maybe some pain they are carrying. The possibilities are endless. Ask them to listen to what Jesus says to them and to respond to him with any questions or disagreements. Instruct the participants to be open and honest with Jesus, even feisty if they need to be. If the setting is outdoors, the dialog with Jesus can be visualized as taking place during a walk.

9. Ask everyone to visualize receiving a symbolic gift from Jesus and to ask what it means.

10. Ask the group members to say good-bye to Jesus in whatever way they choose and, when ready, to come back in their mind to the youth room and open their eyes.

How to Close a Visualization

11. Provide an opportunity to share what went on; this is very important. Almost everybody will share, occasionally choosing to leave out a part of the visualization that's too personal. Sharing validates the experience. Discussing what went on—especially the details about place, greeting, clothing, and the symbolic gift—is necessary for grasping what it all means. Without this shared integration of the visualization, the contents quickly fade and the benefits are lost.

12. Always ask if anyone had difficulty doing the visualization. You and others in the group can then offer advice or encouragement to help that person (or those people) succeed with the visualization the next time.

27

Free to Be Generous:
Unblocking Inhibited Goodness

"People think just because we're teenagers that we don't care, that we're rude and only out for ourselves. Maybe a lot of teens do wear a mask of hardness, but behind the mask a lot more of us really do care than the adult world realizes." I've heard that protest of misunderstood adolescent goodness many times, and I think most youth workers have heard it too. As teens start to like us, they want us to know that there's a lot to like in them too, and there surely is. But teens are keenly aware of the negative youth culture image that clings to them—an image of coldheartedness and selfishness. As youth ministers, we need to be alert to being prejudiced by this image as we begin to form an opinion of and a relationship with young people.

I have formed a definite opinion of the typical adolescent heart that I hope positively responds to their concern for a fair adult response:

The goodheartedness of young people is real. Teens have an idealistic generosity inside them just waiting to be brought out. But the coldness is real too, because young hearts are also vulnerable, and life's hurts can easily plunge them into a self-protective and even cynical hardness.

This chapter proposes a way we can help teens to work with these two inner realities—their goodheartedness and the barriers that block it. The "four zones" is a peer ministry technique designed to get at the hurts that shut down young hearts. The technique helps teens to help one another break out of the hardness that comes from hurt and enables them to release their inner goodness so that in their daily life they can become active and effective for other people.

The hope of easing their accumulation of hurts is sometimes sufficient motivation for teens to want to participate in the four zones activity. But the four zones technique accomplishes that purpose by reaching for an even more powerful motive—the release of the teens' frustrated goodness.

The pitch for the four zones activity goes something like this:

> It may be covered and hidden, but we all have within us a drive to care, to be there, and to be trusted by the other people in our life. That drive is our greatest strength. Today we're giving that strength a name; it's our "active goodness," our "AG." Everybody's AG style is unique, but everyone has one just waiting to be brought out. Our AG is the part of us that wants to serve and looks for ways to do so. We've all experienced it, but it comes and goes.
>
> What prevents our AG drive from kicking in more often, from taking a permanent and prominent place in our personality? AG obviously is the way of Christ, but something holds us back—even if we would like AG to be our way of life.
>
> The barrier is pain. Things happen that hurt us and rob us of any good feelings inside and leave us with nothing for others. We get stuck in self-concern, stuck inside, and we find we just cannot care much beyond ourselves.
>
> The four zones are four distinct parts of daily life that contain four distinct sets of people who are greatly affected by the strength or weakness of our active goodness. And these are the same people who hurt us enough at times to bring our AG to a standstill.
>
> Here are the zones: our home life, our school life, our social life, and our work life. These are the places where

we are called to live out our faith and give out our goodness. These zones contain the groups of people in our life who need us the most and, at times, hurt us the most.

Today we are going to use a prayer technique that will help us free up our ability to be actively good in the four zones of our life.

We give that opening pitch each time we prepare to do the four zones activity. Love for others is established as the key motivator. Hope for one's own healing is neither central nor peripheral; rather, it takes its rightful place as a part of the larger purpose of loving.

After the opening pitch, we break the group into small sharing groups, each with an adult leader. Then one of the adult leaders gives this briefing to the groups:

In your groups you will be asked to share responses to the question "Which zone do I need to visit for prayer so that I can free up my AG?" Please notice that there are four signs in different zones of the room, corresponding with the four zones of your daily life. When you come back from the sharing groups you will be able to go to the zone that you feel is presenting you with difficulty in being good to others.

In the groups, everyone takes a turn deciding, with the help of the others, which zone of their daily life needs prayer attention and what exactly has happened in that zone to cause their heart to shut down.

Before everyone comes back together as a large group, one of our adult leaders places a lit candle on a little table or shelf under each zone sign to light up the signs after the lights are turned off. In addition, we have a large crucifix mounted on a pole that we usually place in the center of the room. Then an adult leader gives these instructions:

When the lights go off and the music comes on, and you feel ready, go to the zone you have chosen and pair up with the first person you find there. Decide who is to be ministered to first. Then sit together on the floor face-to-face, with the person being ministered to facing the cross and the ministering person sitting with her or his back to the cross. The person being ministered to then explains the need. The other person does not offer advice, only questions if needed to help clarify the situation. Next, join hands while the ministering person prays, expressing the thoughts and feelings that come to her or him and reaching for a sense of how the Spirit wants the prayer to go. Both members of the pair may join in the prayer, but the person dealing with the dilemma concentrates mainly on letting the prayers soak in and work. When both people in the pair experience a sense of peace and a feeling that the job is done, physically switch positions and repeat the procedure in the opposite roles.

There is one other zone—the zone of inner life. Not exactly a fifth zone, it's more like the core in the middle of the other four zones. One of our adult leaders gives the instructions for this zone last:

> The inner-life zone is the zone to visit if you're having difficulty being good *to yourself.* A visit to the inner zone might be for people having a hard time liking themselves or for people hurting themselves with drugs, alcohol, or other self-destructive behavior. Or, perhaps, a visit to the inner zone could be good for people who are not eating properly, not keeping in good physical condition, not listening to their need for relaxation, or not keeping a daily time to talk with Christ.
>
> After about fifteen minutes of the four zones, everyone who is not still praying with a partner will gather in that inner-life zone right around the cross, and we will pray a decade of the rosary asking Mary to pray with us for the fullest possible release of our active goodness.

The mechanics of doing the four zones are fairly simple after the first time through. If some people do not find a praying partner in their chosen zone fairly quickly, encourage them to go and grab someone who has not yet gone to any zone to come pray with them.

The four zones is one of our group's newer techniques. We have not used it on a retreat yet, but we do use it every few months or so at a weekly youth meeting. The week after we do the four zones, people are invited to share the results they have seen. And with these stories, as with all witnessing, we encourage one another to take fuller advantage of the power of Christ to strengthen our life.

One young woman, Karen, reported that she had visited the work-life zone because she was bored with her job and her co-workers in the deli department of a supermarket. The day after we prayed, two things opened up for her. The first was a new appreciation for the "salt of the earth" kind of people who serve the public year in and year out in that place. The

second was a switch to the bakery department, where the hours and the work were much better suited to her needs. By the next Sunday's youth meeting, she told us that she was a happy supermarket worker who was able to bring a caring spirit to her customers.

A beloved passage from Paul's letter on love captures the secret of the four zones technique: "So faith, hope, love abide, these three; but the greatest of these is love" (1 Cor. 13:13, RSV). *Faith* might motivate a young person to seek a freed-up heart— "do it, because this is what God wants"—but it will not motivate most teens. And *hope* does motivate some teens—"do it so you'll feel better." However, when *love* is the motive—"do it so you can give freely"—the response is energetic and sustained. As a spiritual motive, love does indeed beat the rest.

The Dark and the Light: A Skit Based on Matthew 5:14–16

This skit can be used to help the young people recognize the active goodness hidden within them and the inhibitions that may be blocking it. The skit can precede or follow the opening pitch to the four zones activity.

Cast

The Girl . . . . . Sarah
The Boy . . . . . Greg
Friend 1 . . . . . Melanie
Friend 2 . . . . . Robbie
The Dark . . . . . Sean
The Light . . . . . Dawn

Girl: (*standing alone*) I had a great life before we moved to this town. The kids here are definitely not my kind of kids. I don't like them, and they don't like me. I hate it here, and I'm stuck here. Everything has gone pretty dark on me. (*enter the Boy and two friends*)

Boy: Hey, dudes, do we have it all or what? A perfect day! . . .

Friend 1: And a day off from school . . .

Friend 2: And plenty of time to hang out at the mall . . .

Boy: And great friends (*motions to the two friends*) and . . . this red balloon (*picks it up*), just meant for me to find. (*blows up the balloon*)

Friend 1: Look! There's that new girl with the red hair.

Friend 2: She acts like we're all scum. I say she's scum!

Boy: No, no, no. The girl is definitely not scum. She's just scared. Oh, this is intense! This is good! See this balloon of happiness that came to us. It will go to her. It will break through her cloud and she will shine.

Friend 2: Greg, don't go over there. She'll slap you down.

Friend 1: Shut up Robbie, Greg is on a roll! (*Action freezes.*) (*enter the Light, dressed in white, and the Dark, dressed in black*)

Dark: Don't do it, Greg. Look at her. She's a geek, a total loser. You'll spoil this perfect day you've got going for you.

Light: Don't listen to that bogus advice, Greg. Underneath that dark mask, she's a great girl. It's an excellent move. Do it!

Boy: Yo, stranger! Here is the balloon of happiness. I give it to you. (*Action freezes again. The Light and the Dark move toward the Girl.*)

Light: Wake up and smell the coffee, girl. He's trying to make friends. Will you lighten up a little and take what he's offering?

Dark: Sure, make friends! He just wants to make fun of you in front of his friends. If you take that balloon, you're dead. His next line will chop you to the ground.

Girl: Thanks (*dramatic pause*) . . . but I don't need your stupid charity. Is my mother paying you to make a fool of yourself or what? (*She pops the balloon with a pin.*) (*exit Light and Dark*)

Boy: Oooooh! (*reels backward to his two friends, who catch him*)

Girl: (*watches, then turns and runs*)

Friend 1: Oh, that hurts!

Friend 2: So, tough guy, you played the hero and she blew you away. How's your perfect day going now?

Boy: Want the truth, friends? (*regains his footing and turns*) That pinprick stung my marvelous personality, and I bleed. But I'm feeling something else too. I feel great—right here. (*indicates heart*) I did the . . . right . . . thing!

Friend 2: What? You're crazy!

Friend 1: Yeah, and that's what's great about you.

Boy: And you know what else? She almost trusted us! I came this close. (*indicates a small space with thumb and fingers*) Next time I will succeed.

Friend 1: I bet you will. You have more light than she has darkness.

28
Crack That Book: Getting into the Scriptural Powerhouse

Sometimes when youth group members use the Bible to lead a meeting or give a talk, an awkward little problem arises. While it would be quite simple to take a pen and mark off the passage right in the Bible, they are not sure that it's okay to write in the Bible. Maybe writing in the Bible is some kind of violation, maybe even a desecration of the Holy Book. I have often seized those moments to say passionately:

> Oh, mark it, please feel free to mark it. Don't you know that a Bible that has been kept crisp and clean and just like new is a thing of sadness to God, like a gift that has never been used? But a Bible that's worn and torn and all marked up is a thing of joy to God. Mark up your Bible all you want. The Bible is yours, make yourself at home in it. That's what it's for and that's what God wants.

Then I admit that I do not have direct revelation that God feels this way but that the beautiful warmth I see in a visibly used Bible convinces me that God really wants us to make the Bible our own.

This chapter contains a series of ideas to help teens see their Bibles as gifts to be used and cared for—making them a bit like the Velveteen Rabbit, who became real only after being loved almost to tatters.

Passage Probing

Give the group a scriptural passage relating to some topic of current concern. Ask them to underline the verse, phrase, or word that has significance for them. Then ask the group members to share what they have underlined and why, and use the sharing as a basis for exploring the topic.

For issues that are more individual, the same technique and passage can be used, but in a slightly different way. Instruct the young people to pray first, asking God to speak to them personally through the Scriptures. The sharing then is not so much a topical discussion as it is a time of witness to the way God's word speaks to each person.

Contradictory Pairs of Passages

When critical thinking on a topic is required, we present the group with pairs of scriptural passages that seem to contradict each other. This forces everyone to get out of the pitfall of literal and mindless use of the Bible and to wrestle with passages until they get at the larger spirit of the Gospel and the relevant truth they need. Here's a troublesome pair we've sharpened our theological teeth on as an example:

"'I am the way and the truth and the life. No one comes to the Father except through me'" (John 14:6, NIV). The passage seems to suggest that people have to formally accept Jesus in order to be saved; this is a favorite belief of fundamentalists. Here's an apparently contradictory passage that seems to say that salvation does not depend on knowing Jesus by name: "'. . . "Lord, when did we see you hungry . . . thirsty . . . a stranger . . . naked . . . sick . . . in prison . . . ?"'

'. . . "Whatever you did for one of the least of these brothers of mine, you did for me"'" (Matt. 25:37–40, NIV). Do you have to be explicitly a Christian to be saved, or do generous deeds also bring us to Christ?

A good contradictory pair of passages about anger is Matt. 5:22 and Mark 5:5.

Praying a Passage

Praying a passage is powerful when a group is wrestling with an issue that deals directly with some aspect of their relationship with Christ. Pick a passage (especially a psalm) that probes the issue at hand, and ask the group members to use the passage for dialoging with Jesus. Instruct them to first tell Jesus where they stand on the issue. Then have them read the first verse of the passage as Jesus' response to their stance. Next, ask them to tell Jesus what his response in this verse triggers in them. To continue the dialog, instruct the group members to look to the second verse for Jesus' reply. Invite them to go through the whole passage, talking and listening, verse by verse. Finally, ask the group members to mark the verses that are the most meaningful to them and, at the end, to report the overall message Christ gave to them.

Practicing a Passage

Ask the group members to pick a passage they have found to be of practical use in their day-to-day life. Then instruct them to write down the scriptural citation and toss it into a common pile. Next, challenge everyone to take a passage from the pile but only if they firmly intend to try to put the passage they pick into practice that week. Unusual is the teen who can resist that challenge. But the challenge is more than a come-on, it gives substance to the act of taking a passage. Tell the group members that they will have an opportunity to report their results the following week, so that they have a sense of accountability as they go home with their passages.

Now, time out for a story that grew out of this technique of practicing a passage. Chuck, a group member who was quite committed but also quite cautious—especially in how he presented himself in the group, picked Luke 14:11, "'For everyone who exalts himself will be humbled, and he who humbles himself will be exalted'" (NIV). The passage is from the story of the self-righteous Pharisee and the humble tax collector. Chuck came back the following week and said: "I like the passage, but I couldn't do anything with it. I couldn't see how to apply it to my life. I'm frustrated with the passage because I feel like I have failed in this exercise." His statement was candid and gutsy; he could have just kept quiet. People applauded. Somebody said: "Chuck, you just practiced your passage. You humbled yourself with us by admitting failure, and we exalted you for your humility." We all laughed and applauded again.

Scriptural Witness

Our group sometimes takes five to ten minutes of a youth meeting to ask for stories in which something from the Scriptures has helped someone solve a problem.

Over the years certain passages have come up again and again as favorites, passages that teens have found to be inspiring and practical in their daily decision-making. I have listed these passages here, along with a word or phrase indicating the kind of issue for which each passage has proven helpful.

Ps. 37:5	indecision
Prov. 3:5–6	confusion
Jer. 29:11–14	apprehension
Matt. 4:7–8	searching
Matt. 6:33	priorities
Matt. 7:3–5	conflict
Matt. 10:19–20	advice
Matt. 11:28–30	overburdened
Luke 6:38	family stress
Luke 18:14	egotism
John 8:31–32	questioning
John 16:24	depression
Eph. 4:25–26,31–32	anger and forgiveness
Phil. 4:6–7	worry
Phil. 4:13	helplessness
1 John 1:9	guilt

Our Personal Gospels Within the Whole Gospel

To begin this activity, we ask the young people to share a passage from their personal gospel. We explain this idea by saying something like the following:

> Certain parts of the Bible are operative for certain persons. We all have particular passages we have stored in our mind like a computer data base that we can call up and use when making decisions. These passages are the gospel we live by. And only the parts of the Bible that we have in storage are really ours, are really the Gospel to us at this point in time. Individuals as well as whole Christian denominations have their own personal gospels. The way we grow in our capacity to live the Gospel is to keep adding to our reserve of passages, not to narrow it down to a set few. The Bible contains more richness than the small amount of it we have gotten hold of so far. And the more passages we can take in and make operative for us, the deeper and richer will be our living of the Christian life.

Your Main Passage

On a retreat we told the young people that Christians each should have a certain passage that's their all-time favorite. It should be a passage that best captures their faith—their sense of what Christ and his message are all about—and it should also be a passage they can fall back on for strength or light when times get tough. I shared that "'. . . Seek, and you will find . . . '" (Matt. 7:7, RSV) has been my main passage ever since I was a teenager because it promises me that any sincere effort to find truth will be rewarded with truth. We asked the young people to identify the passage they found most encouraging or, if they didn't have one yet, to look for one during the retreat.

Two Kinds of "Operative" Passages

Our youth group as a community has its own core gospel, its own set of recurring and operative passages—so can every Christian youth group. For this exercise, ask your group to make a list of the scriptural passages that seem to come up a lot in the group. Then give the following briefing:

> The Bible has two distinct kinds of passages that serve us in two distinct ways—*promise* passages and *commandment* passages. These passages represent the two sides of our covenant with God. Contracts or agreements define what the parties involved are committing themselves to do. And the Bible, which spells out our mutual commitment, our covenant with God, is no different. The Bible lays out the things we can ask of God and the things God can ask of us. Our faith becomes explicit through these two types of passages. Promise passages tell us what we can expect God to do for us, and commandment passages tell us what God expects us to do in the decisions we make.

Then ask the group to refer to the list of operative passages they have generated and to separate the promise passages from the commandment passages.

Some of our group's operative passages follow in three lists—promises, commandments, and combinations of the two. You can refer to them as examples of the operative passages that your group might come up with.

Promises

> ". . . Do not worry about what to say or how to say it. At that time you will be given what to say, for it will not be you speaking, but the Spirit of your Father speaking through you." (Matt. 10:19–20, NIV)

> I can do everything through him who gives me strength. (Phil. 4:13, NIV)

> . . . God is faithful, and he will not let you be tempted beyond your strength, but with the temptation will also

provide the way of escape, that you may be able to endure it. (1 Cor. 10:13, RSV)

"You will receive power when the Holy Spirit comes on you. . . ." (Acts 1:8, NIV)

Commandments

". . . First take the plank out of your own eye, and then you will see clearly to remove the speck from your brother's eye." (Matt. 7:5, NIV)

. . . "'Love the Lord your God with all your heart and with all your soul and with all your mind.' [And] 'love your neighbor as yourself.'" (Matt. 22:37–39, NIV)

"If your brother sins against you, go and show him his fault, just between the two of you. . . ." (Matt. 18:15, NIV)

Be angry, but do not sin. . . . (Eph. 4:26, RSV)

Combinations

We know that in everything God works for good with those who love him, who are called according to his purpose. (Rom. 8:28, RSV)

"For where two or three are gathered in my name, there am I in the midst of them." (Matt. 18:20, RSV)

"Seek first his kingdom and his righteousness, and all these things shall be yours as well." (Matt. 6:33, RSV)

"Come to me, all who labor and are heavy laden, and I will give you rest." (Matt. 11:28, RSV)

"Take my yoke upon you, and learn from me; for I am gentle and lowly in heart, and you will find rest for your souls. For my yoke is easy, and my burden is light." (Matt. 11:29–30, RSV)

Praying the Passionate Psalms

Adolescents are known for their emotional intensity, their ecstatic ups and agonized downs. One book of the Bible stands out for the range and intensity of emotion it expresses—the Psalms, a book of prayers from the heart. And prayer from the heart is the kind of prayer that most young people readily pray and that readily breaks through to the heart of God. In fact, the Gospels contain evidence indicating that Jesus knew the Psalms by heart and prayed them in his times of greatest need.

Each of the psalms listed below expresses an emotional state or situation. You may want to use these steps to lead a prayer exercise on the Psalms:
1. Pick the psalm that most closely matches the emotional state of your heart right now.
2. Pray a line of this psalm out loud.
3. Add a line of your own that builds on the line from the psalm and expresses what you're going through.
4. Pray another line from the psalm out loud.
5. Repeat these steps in alternating fashion all the way through the psalm.

The Passionate Psalms

Psalm 1	peer pressure
Psalm 6	pain
Psalm 22	helplessness
Psalm 23	trust
Psalm 34	crying out for help
Psalm 37	hope
Psalm 38	depression
Psalm 42—43	spiritual longing
Psalm 50	hypocrisy
Psalm 51	guilt
Psalm 62	being under attack
Psalm 91	faced with danger
Psalm 127	working with Christ
Psalm 149	celebrating victory
Psalm 150	joy

I would like to close this chapter with a riddle: Is there anything mentioned in the Bible that is sometimes a sword, a meal, a house, a rock, a lamp, and equipment? Give up? Yes, it's God's word!

> For the word of God is living and active, sharper than any two-edged sword. . . . (Heb. 4:12, RSV)

> ". . . 'Man shall not live by bread alone, but by every word that proceeds from the mouth of God.'" (Matt. 4:4, RSV)

> . . . "If you make my word your home you will indeed be my disciples." (John 8:31, NJB)

> "Therefore everyone who hears these words of mine and puts them into practice is like a wise man who built his house on the rock." (Matt. 7:24, NIV)

Your word is a lamp to my feet . . . (Ps. 119:105, NIV)

All scripture is inspired by God . . . that the man of God may be complete, equipped for every good work. (2 Tim. 3:16–17, RSV)

Do all those references to God's word refer to the actual Scriptures? Many Christians believe that they do. And we Catholics certainly do when we hold up the Scriptures at Mass and say, "This is the word of the Lord." But I believe that the Bible can only become God's word for young people in a personal way when it is approached with a personal openness. Then reading the Scriptures can become a way to overcome what many teens experience as the terrible "silence of God." By helping our young people get the Bible open, we give them the great advantage of making the journey into adulthood in the company of a God who will speak to them intimately every step of the way.

29

You Pray Out Loud?
Getting into Shared Prayer

Opening prayer at our leadership meetings was becoming about as lame as a car firing on two cylinders, so I said: "Praying aloud together is a trademark of our youth community, and I've noticed in these last few leadership meetings that only two of us are doing the praying. I could understand it if you were new members, but you're leaders. If you lose it, everyone will. What's holding you back?"

One person wasn't in the mood, another person couldn't think of anything important enough, another had troubles on his mind. Even as the young people heard their own reasons, they saw that their excuses really amounted to spiritual laziness, and if they were to help group prayer become rich and powerful once again, the laziness needed to be overcome. But Chuck, our oldest leader, had a different sort of reason. "Bob, I don't believe in praying out loud, not just because I prefer to pray privately and silently, but because that's what Jesus actually recommends." Delight twinkled in Chuck's eye as he posed his challenge, and a look of shock crossed everyone else's face. Chuck meant every word he spoke, but he had been around long enough to know what the others weren't so sure of—that I would welcome his challenge and we would get a great discussion out of it.

Chuck went on, bold as brass:

> Matthew 6:1 of the Revised Standard Version reads: "Beware of practicing your piety before men in order to be seen by them; for then you will have no reward from your Father who is in heaven." Verse 6, "But when you pray, go into your room and shut the door and pray to your Father who is in secret; and your Father who sees in secret will reward you." Jesus says not to pray aloud with others, Bob.

Other heads around the room were beginning to nod in agreement.

And now the debate was on in earnest. "If you pray just to look good to others, Chuck, then you should indeed shut your mouth. That's the problem Jesus is going after."

"But why does he say, 'When you pray, go into your room and shut the door'?"

"Because that's a good thing to do too, a real good thing. Jesus is talking about having your own daily prayer time. He doesn't exclude praying with others."

"But you can't help thinking about how your prayers affect others when you pray aloud."

"Right, and the effect will be a good effect if you're sincerely praying and not just trying to make an impression. Honest prayer inspires honest prayer. Praying out loud is a great gift to any group."

"Okay, but when did Jesus ever say to pray aloud together?" Chuck was after me relentlessly and loving every minute of it.

"I don't think he ever gave instructions about praying aloud, except if you count the instruction to say the whole Lord's Prayer in the plural rather than in the singular—'Our Father,' not 'my Father.'"

"Weak, Bob, weak."

"Okay, here's something better. What if Jesus himself prayed aloud in front of others and explained the value of it? Would that satisfy you?"

Up until now, Chuck had been scoring well and looking confident, but suddenly his smile got sheepish, "Did he really pray like that?" He knew I had him, as I dramatically opened the Bible to John 11:41–42 and read aloud:

"Father, I thank you for hearing my prayer.
I myself knew that you hear me always,
but I speak
for the sake of all these who are standing around me,
so that they may believe it was you who sent me." (NJB)

Then I said, ruthlessly: "Here and in a number of other places in the Gospels, Jesus prays aloud, and he says here that he does so because he wants people to hear him praying so that they can see directly how he relates to God and have their faith built up."

Chuck's smile was big now. "You win, Bob. I wanted to see if you could convince me, and you did. I guess we had better start getting our praying together back into gear."

So great was Chuck's influence that before long, the leadership group became an inspiration to pray with: the realness of their prayer brought a real sense of Christ's presence that would come over us like a wave after we had been praying for a while.

I replay that whole exchange in this chapter because Chuck articulates so well the resistances people feel when it comes to praying out loud with other people. Chuck's challenge gave me a chance to answer those resistances, and they are well worth overcoming. In fact, many of our young people have reported that when they first came to the youth group, they were touched and inspired most powerfully by the sound and feeling of people praying openly together. They have also reported how strange and unusual the experience was, but the openness of the praying had an appeal they could not deny.

The Power of Shared Prayer

In this section of the chapter, I will describe several practical methods our youth group has developed for praying together that fit comfortably into our meetings and activities. And I will begin by describing an occasion when praying with a young person in our group gave me the key to a difficult situation that I couldn't figure out how to resolve by myself.

The big basement room in the parish center was starting to fill up with exuberant young people turning out for one of our seasonal youth dances. I was the busy youth coordinator, deftly managing dozens of last-minute details, when someone quietly approached me and mentioned that at the previous dance some of our members had sneaked in without paying. I glanced around with anger in my eyes and spotted two likely suspects who had earlier come in the back door, ostensibly helping the DJ with his equipment. I strolled over and asked to see if their hands had the magic marker stroke showing that they had paid. One lad grinned triumphantly as he held out his marked hand. But the other gave me the stricken look of someone whose integrity had just been called into question. That look stuck, vibrating in me like a knife as I walked away.

I should have known that my question would wound the passionate dignity of that young man, and sure enough I had blown it, and he was deeply offended. Now my ability to be the relaxed, welcoming youth minister was totally shot. My friendliness was a mask with nothing behind it but distress and guilt. So I went to Paul, one of the older youth group members, and spilled out my story. We were standing off in a corner, and when I had told my tale, he unobtrusively said a short prayer for me. While I listened to his prayer, it came to me strong and clear that I had to go back and tell the young man I had hurt exactly how badly I felt about it.

The reception I got was totally unexpected: "Bob, you don't need to apologize. Yes, I was hurt, but when you left I asked my friend about it and found out that you were right. He and several others did sneak in last time. They're the ones I'm mad at, not you." And with that, my heart's load was lifted, and I could move freely back into the joys of ministry and into the dancing all around me.

The act of praying together had opened my distressed spirit to the gentle nudging of God's Spirit. I could not have responded positively to the situation alone. I needed someone to help me ask for God's guidance and help me listen to God's response. I needed the added power that flows from linking up spiritual batteries in prayer.

Ways of Praying Together

Praying down the Spirit: We pray down the Spirit right before all sorts of events—dances, trips, youth meetings, talks. People simply think for a moment about all the good things they hope will happen in the upcoming event and then turn these hopes into prayers. For example, someone might pray for "a spirit of trust and joy among us" or "a talk that really challenges all of us." In our need, we throw open a door for whatever blessings God is waiting to be invited to give us.

Popcorn prayer: Popcorn prayers are one-word or one-phrase prayers that are easier to say out loud than longer prayers. Lots of themes are possible. The word can express praise—what we love about God. The word can express thanks for the ways we feel we've been blessed. The word can express repentance—what we are sorry for and need to strengthen in our daily life. The word can express a petition—what we hope for.

Opening prayer at meetings: The group leader begins a meeting by welcoming Christ and then inviting the group to offer thanks for any unacknowledged gifts they've received from him. After that step, the leader invites the group to ask for new things they need from Jesus. Sometimes in groups just learning to pray together, members can get ready for prayer by jotting down two lists of items—thankings and askings. Or people can pair off briefly and help each other decide which prayers need to be brought out. The depth and intensity of what people offer in prayer has a domino effect in moving and freeing other people to pray.

Praying with people: People prayer can go on between just two people when one (or both) of them has a need. Or it can be used in a group to pray for one of its members, maybe by stopping the regular proceedings occasionally to pray in response to a need that has arisen suddenly. Or a large group can gather around and pray for a smaller group, with a laying on of hands. For instance: a large group can pray for a team that is about to plan an event for that large group.

Whatever the configuration of people, the format of the prayer is always the same. The prayee first explains the situation of need. The pray-er simply listens and, if necessary, asks questions to clarify the situation. The pray-er must resist the temptation to give advice. Once the problem is out in the open, the pray-er begins praying so that Christ can be the problem solver. If a group is doing the praying, a designated leader launches the praying and then lets the group run with it, praying the prayers that come to them until the leader senses the job is done. In this kind of prayer, the prayees often report feeling much love and peace coming to them through the feeling of joined hands and the sound of the voices, and often they hear things in the prayer that become for them the voice of Christ.

All four methods of praying together are ended with the Lord's Prayer, a Hail Mary, or a Glory Be. We normally take hands when we pray together to express a united effort. The tone of the praying can range all the way from serious to playful, from tearful to joyful. Unless something very gripping is happening, we keep all four kinds of praying together fairly brief.

Several other ways of praying out loud as a group are described elsewhere in this book. See chapters 16, 17, 22, and 30.

What does all this praying accomplish, besides giving people a good feeling? Well, that good united feeling is itself a great gift not to be taken for granted. And the constant reinforcement of the practice of prayer is an obvious and practical benefit. We have noticed that the quality of our group experiences clearly sinks whenever we are foolish or embarrassed enough to omit putting ourselves in the hands of Christ by praying together at the outset.

The effects that flow from praying aloud as a group are quite obvious to anyone who is willing to see the good results. But a final effect, one that Jesus hints at, has to be inferred and just taken on faith: When we are unashamed to honor God in front of one another, we give God a happiness that is akin to the happiness parents feel when their children give back love and gratitude and hold them in a place of honor.

Jesus suggests this proud parental joy when he says, "'Every one who acknowledges me before men, I also will acknowledge before my Father who is in heaven'" (Matt. 10:32, RSV). Our courage to overcome whatever tries to silence our faith will result in Jesus showing us off to God in heaven. And I think Jesus will be happy to show off youth groups who have the courage publicly, in prayer, to acknowledge his presence.

30

Four Corners: Repairing Broken Hearts

The Preparation

Saturday night is the climactic time of weekend retreats. The message is now mostly delivered. Trust has developed, and the time is psychologically right for breakthrough.

Some planners like to do a reconciliation service. Others like a healing service. And still others prefer a recommitment service. We used to use variations of those themes, something a little different each time, until we hit upon an approach that does it all. We call the approach "four corners," and it has become so popular that for eight years now, it has been our Saturday night plan, no matter what else is happening. People talk about and anticipate doing the four corners weeks before a retreat, and afterward, they talk about it weeks and even months later, remembering the remarkable things they experienced.

The retreat program shifts into four-corner mode shortly after the Saturday evening meal. To begin, someone gives a brief witness talk about something Christ did for them during a previous four corners.

Here is one story we heard from a sophomore named Ellen. I am using her own words (with just a little editing):

I never imagined anything like this could happen to me. To begin with, I wasn't getting anything out of the retreat or four corners. I was in a bad mood, but I felt drawn to the faith corner. I knew something was going on, and I just wanted to be there. I half-knew my down mood had to do with my brother Ricky, who had died when I was five, but when I got to the corner, my problem suddenly became very clear. I wasn't sure Ricky knew I really loved him as much as I did, and I wasn't confident of his love for me. Other people were in the faith corner praying about their own things, but there was a strong feeling of support for one another. I started crying. A great feeling came over me. I could feel God telling me, "It's all right." And I felt Ricky's love for me. The empty space in me wasn't there anymore—just God's peace. There was so much healing in that corner. We were all close, more than close. We were all connected; everyone's heart was being healed.

Since then, every time I feel myself doubting, I think about that experience. It was my first encounter with the Holy Spirit. The encounter had a profound effect on my faith. And it was all just given to me without my working at it. Since then I've learned to look for it, and when I need to, I think about something that's hurting me and offer it up to God.

Stories like Ellen's generate feelings of expectancy within the retreat community, but we tell the participants that a lot depends on how well they prepare, how openly they come, how real they are willing to be with God.

Then we send the group members off to prepare for their four-corner experience with some journal work (see chapter 19). The focus of the journal writing is always on the burdens people carry, the layer of trouble that blocks joy and hampers freedom. For example: "Dear Jesus, here's how it feels to be me these days . . ." Or, "Dear Jesus, here's what I must deal with in my own heart if I am to be free to give your love to others . . ."

We instruct everyone to list the titles of the four corners —*Faith, Healing, Peace, Forgiveness*—along the top of a page in their journal. We ask the participants, as they are writing their journal entry, to circle the words that best express the needs they are finding. The journal time usually lasts about fifteen minutes.

Next, we tell everyone to get together with their "families," the small groups that already have met several times during the weekend to discuss talks. The families have about forty-five minutes to complete these four tasks:

1. Everyone shares what struck home with them about the witness talk.
2. Veteran retreatants explain the mechanics of the four corners to first-timers.
3. Veterans share additional stories about experiences they've had in the corners.
4. Everyone shares their travel plans—which corners they plan to visit and why.

Perhaps the preparation seems overdone—a witness talk, journal writing, and then family discussions, all to get ready for one little prayer service. But preparation is the main ingredient. The four corners approach owes its power to all the listening, writing, and talking we do beforehand. These labors enable all of us to get in touch with our private agendas, which otherwise would remain only vaguely defined and would be too hard to work with.

Once we know our needs, we're in a good position to let our Lord touch and relieve these burdened hearts we lug around with us. "'Blessed are the pure in heart, for they shall see God'" (Matt. 5:8, RSV). That verse applies not only the purity that follows Christ's touch but also the honest awareness of need that permits us to seek that touch. And it is the humble purity of letting ourselves know our deep need for Christ that is the goal of the preparation phase of the four corners.

The Rite

The hard ground in our hearts has been plowed up. Rich soil has now been turned over, but along with it, plenty of rocks and weeds have surfaced. The retreat and the preparation phase of the four corners have led us to an openhearted state, and we now move to the chapel (or main meeting room if there is no suitable chapel).

We enter the chapel in silence; a single candle on the altar lights our way. The hush is holy, the atmosphere charged with expectancy. In each corner of the chapel, signs with large letters are dimly visible, identifying each of the four corners: in the front, near the tabernacle, *Faith;* in the other front corner, *Healing;* in the rear corners, *Peace* and *Forgiveness.* And on a little table or stand beneath each sign, waits a single unlit candle.

We sing a few songs, the ones we pray best with. And we sing the songs to Christ, letting the tide of faith and hope rise among us as we reach toward his love. Then the four corners moderator (an adult leader) picks up the single altar candle and, by its light, reads the "four corners verse." The verse is John 16:24, "'Until now you have not asked for anything in my name. Ask and you will receive, and your joy will be complete'" (NIV). The moderator then explains the verse, with conviction, and presents it as a challenge:

> Jesus is not happy with his followers. They have needs, but their needs remain unmet because they hang onto them and do not dare to ask Jesus for help. He urges them, "Ask!" Why? Because only then does Jesus' desire to bless get fulfilled. We, like the disciples in John 16:24, frustrate that desire most of the time. Jesus wants to heal and forgive and build faith and grant peace much more than we want him to. But tonight give him joy by letting him give you joy. Let him in deep. Ask deep. Be bold and be real with him. Let him do great things for you and in you.

After the moderator has issued the challenge, the corner captains go with their teams to their respective corners. (The corner teams are composed of veteran retreatants who station themselves in their respective corners to be available to those individuals who want to come and pray with them.) Then the moderator gives these final instructions:

> Go to the corner of your choice when you see a team member who is free to pray with you, or go with someone from the group with whom you want to pray. Work from your travel plans, but let the Spirit override those plans if new needs surface. Tell the person you've chosen to pray with why you've come and what you need, and then go right to prayer—no advice, just prayer. Usually just the corner-team person, or the person you have chosen to pray with, prays, but join in if you wish. Pray until you feel the need is met and then go to the next corner or back to a pew. The sacrament of reconciliation is available in the side room.

The corner teams have been praying quietly while these instructions are given—and actually they have also been doing *palanca* all week (see chapter 9). Now the moderator takes the candle from the altar, holds it high, and says: "Christ is one, but he comes to us now in four ways to satisfy four hungers of our hearts. He calls to us in these four ways. Hear his call."

The moderator carries the altar candle toward the faith corner and is met by the corner captain, who brings out the unlit corner candle to be lit by the altar candle. Returning to the faith corner, the captain reads the "Call to Faith." (The text for the corner calls is given at the end of the chapter.) Then the corner captain carries the faith candle halfway up the side aisle to meet and light the peace candle. The peace corner captain then carries the lighted peace candle back to the peace corner to read the "Call to Peace." After that, the peace corner captain carries the peace candle halfway across the back aisle to meet and light the forgiveness candle, and so on, until all four candles have been lit and all four calls have been issued.

Then the gentle music of John Michael Talbot starts playing, and people begin to move—slowly at first—to the various corners, where they speak quietly and then pray earnestly. Soon all the corner teams are busy, as people travel to the now-externalized territories of their inner selves. Tears and laughter can be heard occasionally amidst the undercurrent of intimate talk, to one another and to God.

We keep Kleenex handy in each corner, and soon the floor is littered. We usually pray with hands joined and conclude with a good hug. Sometimes the whole transaction happens in a hug. Adults and youth are both pray-ers and prayees. We usually ask anyone who seems stuck in a pew how they are doing with their plans. Sometimes prayers for courage or other needs are prayed in the pews if the corner seems too long a step—but that's rare.

About forty-five minutes later, when most people seem finished, the leader starts the Lord's Prayer and everyone else joins in. The Lord's Prayer brings four corners to a close.

Not until the next day, at the witness time that concludes the retreat, do we begin to find out the good things that happened for people on Saturday night. Hates have been dissolved. Christ has become real. A sense of God's power has often physically been felt, flowing sometimes as a distinctly felt energy, a tingling, or a trembling—astonishing, delighting, healing. Sometimes a corner person will report praying words that seemed to come from someone else. The stories are fun to hear and fun to tell, but it is a fun filled with serious-ness, and perhaps the better word for it is *joy*. "'Ask, . . . that your joy may be full'" (John 16:24, RSV): The asking has been risked, and the fullness has been given.

The Call to Faith

After lighting the faith candle, the faith corner person reads aloud the following call:

> Loving a God we can't see is hard. Living for a Jesus we often can't feel is hard. Faith is a struggle for everyone. But Jesus rewards our efforts. For every step we take toward him, he takes ten toward us. Ask him, he will help you to trust him more and more.
>
> Jesus' disciples said, "Increase our faith." And Jesus did so. Here in this corner he's waiting to increase your faith, too.
>
> Come if you feel far from the Lord, and let him draw you near.
>
> Come if you've turned away from the Lord and want to turn back. You will give him and yourself great joy.
>
> Come even if you doubt he's real, and if you seek him with all your heart, you will find him.
>
> Come if you aren't as committed to Jesus as you would like to be, and ask him again to let you be his.
>
> Come if you have just used Jesus to do things for you and want to tell him you love him.
>
> Come if you want to turn over to Jesus some area of your life you have held back, and let his will be your way.
>
> Come if you have been angry with God and want to feel his love and trust in his love again.

The Call to Peace

After lighting the peace candle, the peace corner person reads aloud the following call:

> Sometimes people do terrible things to us and hurt us so deeply that peace seems forever out of reach. Sometimes we harden ourselves, stop caring, and pull back behind walls and masks. We can become so lost in ourselves and so cut off from others that no power on earth can find us.
>
> The Prince of Peace calls to you. He knows where you are. He says, "Receive my peace now, tonight. Come to me in the peace corner."
>
> Come if you're holding a grudge against someone. Let Jesus melt you and free you to forgive.
>
> Come if you have someone to apologize to and have been putting it off. Jesus will give you courage.

Come if you are at odds with a parent or brother or sister or other family member, and let Jesus reawaken your love.

Come if you've been cold and mean to someone in the community instead of talking things out. Come alone or come together, and ask Jesus for the gift of friendship.

Come if people you love are at odds with each other, and offer yourself to Jesus for the gift of their renewed friendship.

Come if your soul knows no rest, and you need the quieting touch of Jesus. Let him draw you down into his deep peacefulness.

Come if the troubles of our world worry you, and ask Jesus to make your life an instrument of his peace.

The Call to Forgiveness

After lighting the forgiveness candle, the forgiveness corner person reads aloud the following call:

We hurt people. We hurt ourselves. Our selfishness takes over so easily and so often, and our sins hurt Jesus too. So we back away and feel unworthy, unchristian, and unable. But Jesus says, "Wait. Don't run from me. I'm not here to punish." He longs to forgive you and set you on your feet again.

Jesus said, "Father forgive them," and in this corner that's just what he wants to do for you.

Come if you judged anyone as less worthy than yourself with gossip or harsh words, and let Jesus touch your attitude.

Come if you acted against yourself or the community with drinking or drugs; Jesus wants to forgive you.

Come if Jesus has been calling you to go to confession and you've resisted him. Let Jesus gently encourage and strengthen you.

Come if you have been rude to your parents or have lied to them or have ignored their authority, and let Jesus bring you back to them.

Come if you've gone too far with sex or indulged in sexually immoral entertainment. Jesus will welcome your repentance.

Come if you've participated in seances or used Ouija boards or anything of the occult, and let Jesus' Holy Spirit clear your body and soul of any other spirit but your own and his.

Come if you've given in to jealousy or resentment or stealing; Jesus longs to shower down his forgiveness on you and make you clean.

The Call to Healing

After lighting the healing candle, the healing corner person reads aloud the following call:

Everybody's got pain. There's no need to hide it. There's no shame in saying you're hurting. Jesus is calling you to open up your pain to him. He wants to touch you and help you. Maybe you thought nothing could help. Well, you were wrong about that.

Jesus says, "I came to heal the brokenhearted." Here in this corner he will do just that.

Come if you don't like yourself very much, and let Jesus rebuild your self-respect.

Come if you're hurting because a relationship has ended; let Jesus comfort your heart.

Come if someone close to you has died and you haven't let go; let Jesus fill the loss with his love.

Come if some social experience has put you down and made you feel worthless, and let Jesus restore your confidence.

Come if you have a fear or a shyness that blocks the real you, and let Jesus free you to give yourself to others.

Come if you have a physical problem and put yourself in the care of Jesus, the Great Physician.

Come if you're stuck in an attitude or habit you just can't break; let Jesus free you to be yourself again.

31

To Belong, to Be, to Care, to Do: Responding to the Evolving Spiritual Needs of Youth Group Members

For a long time, I wished that someone would come up with a handy list of the changes teens go through during their high school years in a youth group. Adolescent development theory helped a little, but it bunched the changes it saw too vaguely into early, middle, or late adolescence. And besides, I also wanted to know what spiritual possibilities would appropriately match each of the changes in each of the high school years.

In the late seventies, I heard a study described that was specific enough to suit me. The study reported that teens only become ready to experience the otherness of God for themselves late in their sophomore year. Before that, their developmental concerns are focused too exclusively within the boundaries of self to allow for any looking beyond.

Using that clue, I then did some experimenting and watching in our youth group and gradually saw a whole series of other readinesses appear year by year. Putting them all together, I found I had my little schema. In this chapter, I present a portrait of youth group high schoolers and their spiritual potential as freshmen, sophomores, juniors, and seniors.

The language I have chosen for this sequence of changes is purposely nonpsychological and down-to-earth so that it can be used directly with the young people to help them think about what they are going through. Everyone travels the path uniquely, of course, but it does help to have a road map of the geography ahead in order to recognize each new phase of the journey as it comes along.

My map consists of the developmental concerns that emerge at each grade level. I will present four stories, each about a young person grappling with the characteristic issues of his or her developmental stage. The stories will include the decisive and appropriate spiritual step each young person took in order to successfully resolve the issue he or she faced.

Freshmen

Freshmen stand at the very end of childhood, and so also do eighth, seventh, and even sixth graders. Because rates of development vary so greatly in early adolescence, the freshman concerns I will describe have actually been kicking in all through the middle school years. By freshman year, however, everybody is experiencing the same predominant concern—peer acceptance.

Here's how it works. Over the course of several years, these young people have grown physically, they have become sexually mature, and they have developed a new mental quickness. But they are nonetheless still children. For several years, some of their dependence on the family has been shifting to the peer group, but dependence it still is. Moving into the peer world brings not so much an independence as it does a loosening of the exclusive family dependence, and that shift represents a preparation for, a foreshadowing of, the truly independent sense of self yet to come.

At the freshman level, the peer bond takes on new importance, not at all replacing the crucial home influence, but weighing in as a second major identity-shaper. Identity in the freshman peer world is not so much a question of *who you are* as *who you're with*.

Peer influence at the freshman level can work for great good, or it can work for great evil, especially when parents and family fail to stay in close touch with their rapidly changing young teens. And parents and family can easily lose touch when, for instance, they misread newly distinct peer identity choices and newly critical responses to family "givens" as a message that the home influence is no longer wanted or needed. In reality, parents and other key adults are still the primary transmitters of values and are very much needed as coaches to help teens figure out how to apply sound values to their developing peer relationships.

Without such guidance from parents and other key adults, the peer world of teens can exert a terrible conformist and heart-suppressing tyranny on freshmen, who have a deep and normal need to find peer acceptance. And yet, when freshmen come into a well-guided high school youth group of mixed ages, where kindness and mutual respect are perceived as the norm, that same need for acceptance can bring freshmen to a very positive bonding with older young people, who will call forth unique expression and growth, and point them toward a unique sense of self soon to come. That, of course, is what a youth group can offer—as this story illustrates:

Matt initially came to the youth group for only one reason: Elaine. She lived outside of town, and joining the group was the only way he could see her. Matt had no interest in the group as such. He fully expected to find a bunch of nice, quiet religious types. But that narrow image was soon blown away. Matt found jocks and theater buffs, honors students and struggling students, rowdy people and shy people. Later Matt took the plunge and told the group why he had come and what he had expected. He had us laughing at the sheer boldness and humanness of what he was revealing of himself. Then he said, "But really, this group is awesome; everyone is different, and you all get along."

Matt had been in teen groupings comprised of just one type of person, and he wanted to break out of that rut, so he decided to stick around for a while—even though he ended up going out with someone else. Matt's big move, instead of just hanging out with jocks and wearing the jock mask, was accepting our challenge to be honest and real, instead of being a "type." He sealed that decision when he told the group what had gone on inside him. That dropping of the mask and opening up is the first major step we invite freshmen to take. My motto for this first spiritual challenge is, "Be yourself with others."

It is healthy for freshmen to hear that challenge from Jesus as well. Jesus reserved some of his harshest words for the Pharisees, whose concern for peer approval dominated them completely.

"[The Pharisees] do all their deeds to be seen by men; . . . they love the place of honor at feasts and the best seats in the synagogues, and salutations in the market places, . . . [but they] are like whitewashed tombs, which outwardly appear beautiful, but within they are . . . full of hypocrisy and iniquity." (Matt. 23:5–7, 27–28, RSV)

Sophomores

At some point during the sophomore year of high school, the adult is born. Richard Reichert, a well-known writer on adolescent catechesis, told youth ministers at the 1985 New England Consultants on Youth Ministry Conference at Boston University that he's gotten so he can pinpoint with many sophomores the exact two-week period when it happens. The shell of childhood gets broken, and out steps the brand-new baby adult. And this new adult's big concern is, Will anybody notice?

Parents, teachers, and even friends often take a painfully long time to recognize the change in sophomores and to shift their modes of relating with them. Unlike freshmen, sophomores need more than just to be in the play, band, or team; they need to make a contribution that is noticed. Unlike freshmen, sophomores need more than just to have friends; they want to be recognized by their friends as unique and worthwhile persons.

Psychologists see this time as the start of a new developmental stage, which they call the "stage of romanticism"—a time of exuberant discovery of people, of ideals, of life, of self. And some research indicates that this is the year they can discover God.

The sophomore year can be a year of joy, if all goes well, but it also can be a year of deep and bitter disappointment. Some sophomores give up on their new sense of self before they ever really get the lid off. Much depends on whether, as newborn adults, they find any welcome in their world.

When this need for individual expression and recognition focuses on faith, the commonly accepted belief in Christ that they grew up with is now no longer adequate. The challenge they willingly accept is to seek and find Christ for themselves—person to Person, friend to Friend—and then to build a unique and real relationship, allowing him to unlock and bring out their hidden gifts, their inner selves.

For Jason, a sophomore in our youth group, an academic need brought his spiritual challenge into focus. He always used to panic and blank out during tests. Consequently, even though he had studied thoroughly, he always did poorly. Jason knew he had it in himself to perform much better, but he was stuck. Jason had heard a lot of people talk pretty openly in youth meetings about their encounters with Christ as a "friend you can turn to." So before tests, Jason began to pray for calmness. He got it, and his grades shot up dramatically. Now he had his own story to tell—and he told it enthusiastically—about how Christ came through for him and freed up his real abilities. And this is spiritual step number two: In a group that's open about their experiences with Christ, people can gradually learn to let him bring out their new capabilities, their new selves. The call we issue to sophomores is, "Be your best with Christ."

We can perhaps think of Peter as something of a delayed sophomore, clumsily calling attention to himself, yet with an appealing kind of exuberance. In his first encounter with Jesus, Peter, as a simple fisherman, was overwhelmed by his own inadequacy and said, "'Go away from me, Lord; I am a sinful man'" (Luke 5:8, NIV). But Jesus replied by naming the kind of person Peter had it in him to be, "'Don't be afraid; from now on you will catch men'" (Luke 5:10, NIV).

Some Conclusions

Before moving on to the juniors and seniors, some conclusions about the freshmen and sophomores are in order. In pastoral terms, we have been talking about pre-evangelization and evangelization. Our mission to the acutely self-conscious freshmen is to provide conditions that allow them to relax and be themselves at church. This is an enormous spiritual step, and the relief it brings is enormous as well. And this really is pre-evangelization—getting comfortable in the vicinity of God's people.

Our mission to the newly emerging individuality of sophomores is to provide conditions that encourage them to seek and find Christ for themselves as the Friend who will help them set free the person and the gifts within. This is evangelization—getting people to interact with Christ.

At this point, halfway through their four high school years, if they have taken up the challenges we have offered them, our young pilgrims on the Catholic spiritual journey can now claim two spiritual territories as their own—church as a real comfort and Jesus as a real companion.

That pair of steps may seem like a lot for anyone to accomplish, and it is. But it's not enough yet to constitute discipleship. Many people meet Jesus in the Gospels, as did blind Bartimaeus, ". . . And immediately he received his sight . . ." But after the benefits of meeting Jesus are received, not everyone responds as Bartimaeus did, ". . . and followed [Jesus] on the way" (Mark 10:52, RSV). The number of our newly freed up young believers who will actually decide to live out the Christian life in their junior and senior years remains to be seen.

A Caution

Before we follow our young travelers into junior year territory, let's step back and look at this total process from the viewpoint of parishioners. We might ask, "Isn't this sequence of spiritual changes being presented simply conversion, and can't conversion take place at any age and stage of life? Why tie conversion so tightly to adolescent development and focus so much of the energy and time of youth ministry toward it at this period in the young people's lives?"

I propose that for Catholics baptized as infants, conversion, when it happens in adult life, often entails some backtracking, some undoing and reforming of views, values, and habits that were wrongly shaped in the adolescent years when the basic identity decisions were first made. So attention to and care for these outlined steps will help teens get their views, values, and habits headed in the right direction the first time around. And we help the young people by taking seriously and naming clearly the decisions they face at this time in their life.

But a further concern must be weighed by anyone considering such a conversion model in the parish's high school youth ministry program. Does the adult community embrace this model and give priority to prayer, scripture, and a Christ-centered spirituality? If so, you have adults who can help make the model work. If so, you have a parish leadership (lay and clerical) who can authorize, commission, and support such a ministry effort. If not, you should not be tempted to do this kind of youth work just because the ideal is personally appealing. This model works successfully only when the adult parish embraces it and supports it.

Now, back to our young pilgrims where we left them—midway through their four-year youth group journey.

The spiritual growth steps of freshmen and sophomores represent a partial conversion. Good relations have been opened up with the church and with Christ. They're actively getting acquainted, but no commitments have been made. Commitment happens in the strenuous reality-testing of the junior and senior years.

Juniors

The junior year is a time of great storm and struggle. Still fresh from the discovery of self and others (and even Christ), the new adults must now face a series of tough adult choices that will establish them firmly in their own particular set of values. These are life-shaping decisions, and they are not made in a vacuum of calm reflection. Agonizing personal and interpersonal crises seem to be the norm for juniors, crises that force these first major adult decisions.

With hurricane force, life comes breaking in on them and says, "Choose how you will treat yourself, your friends, love, sex, money, and commitment." And these choices must not be regarded as merely the growing pains of big children, they must be taken seriously as critical turning points in the formation of adult character. Adult consequences will follow their decisions. Precedents are being set, and personal policies are being formed.

As juniors face these formative crises, they need to hear the Gospel addressed to them personally—or more precisely, applied to each particular situation that comes up. If they face each situation squarely, let the Gospel challenge them, and pray their way to Christ's method of handling crises, a wonderful result will follow, something more than the peace that normally accompanies the practice of the Gospel. The juniors' newly decisive and grounded Christianity will make them each a powerhouse of good influence in the group. They will sense this power, and others will sense it. Personal gifts will suddenly become potent ministries capable of reshaping the life of the group. And, of course, some juniors will now decide against the Gospel lifestyle, and they will often just stop coming to the group.

Here is the story of a junior named Cindi and the crisis that resulted from the way she treated herself. As a freshman, Cindi's warm and outgoing nature fit right in with the style of the youth group. As a sophomore, Cindi had a powerful and persuasive experience of Christ. Her growth was strong and consistent. Then, as a junior, Cindi ran into trouble. Alongside her growing love for Christ and others, a stubborn streak of self-hate persisted. Cindi would never allow anything good to be said about herself—she just couldn't accept affirmation from anyone. The force of her experience of Christ's love for her gradually brought about a showdown. She was finally able to name this very unchristian treatment of herself as sin and then give it up in the sacrament of reconciliation.

Then, feeling a sudden great relief about herself, Cindi saw with new clarity the value of every person. And more, she

saw the attitude of self-put-down crippling the hearts of lots of her peers and hobbling their ability to love. Suddenly, Cindi went on a rampage in the group, exuberantly teaching people to look for and point out what's beautiful in one another and, by God, to believe what they heard. Thanks to her, candid affirmation became a trademark of the group.

Cindi discovered the special influence that juniors can wield. In groups that invite peer leadership and ministry, juniors find that if they decide to let Christ shape their values, they will have great power to shape the group. The challenge to juniors is, "Take charge in the group."

The Gospel of Luke offers a parallel to Cindi's story. Peter's great crisis of character came the night he denied Jesus three times. Just before it happened, Jesus prepared him with words that might just as well be spoken to juniors: "'Simon, Simon! Look, Satan has got his wish to sift you all like wheat; but I have prayed for you, Simon, that your faith may not fail, and once you have recovered, you in your turn must strengthen your brothers'" (Luke 22:31–32, NJB).

Our juniors will just as surely be soul-sifted, and it's good for them to know it, lest like Peter they think their untried religious zeal is enough. It is also good for our juniors to know that they can count on us to pray them through the spiritual vulnerabilities they discover in themselves. And, once they get through that unavoidable rough stretch of the journey, they can come to a firmed-up capacity to strengthen their brothers and sisters—just like Peter did.

Seniors

Seniors have two compelling concerns: the future and how to face it, and the past and how to leave it. Strategies for making it in the adult world—for example, which school to attend, which career path to take—are constantly on their mind. And seniors are always feeling the impact of the end of, or change in, all the relationships and comforts they have gained during their growing-up years.

Together the two concerns are a lot to carry, a lot to deal with. What seniors are going through is so different from what other people, younger or older, are feeling that seniors can feel strangely disconnected from the familiar scenes of home, school, work, and church. Some seniors plunge into partying. Some cling to old roles and pretend nothing is changing. Some quietly disengage. Some become vaguely angry. One enormous reality is forcing itself in on them: childhood is over, and they have to move on.

The challenge to seniors is a call to courage—courage to make plans that do more than just cope with the adult realities, courage to make plans for an adulthood based on their best dreams and gifts. The call to courage also challenges seniors to face their strong feelings about letting go and to keep dealing with them instead of trying to escape them.

When seniors can find the poise to deal with the deep grieving and the deep hoping that are both stirring within them, their unlocked heart can bring out a third kind of courage—the courage to live generously, that is, to care with some degree of passion about how other people are doing and not just about oneself. We challenge seniors to be ambitious for the good of others around them just as much as for themselves, and thus to grow in the special freedom and the special happiness that only that life posture can give.

A young woman named Laurie once gave us a fine example of that kind of courage: In her senior year, Laurie still came faithfully to the weekly youth meeting, but she pulled back from specific leadership roles to allow time for her non-youth-group friends. This was her last year with them as well, and she did not want to neglect any of her important relationships at this critical time.

Laurie's social style was quiet and candid, and within the group she left no doubt that she cared a lot about people, with a gutsy kind of honesty. Laurie was working well with her "senior stresses" and consequently did have enough poise to bring her gift of caring and honesty to a situation that confronted her one afternoon in the library.

Laurie sat near three girls who were teasing and embarrassing a socially awkward boy, sending him notes that one of them liked him and "wanted his body." Laurie walked over and told them, "I see what you're doing and it really stinks, so quit it." And they did. She reported this story with flashing eyes, but behind her indignation, she (and all of us) felt delight in her deed. This ability to focus Christlike anger and stick up for others can emerge beautifully in seniors. Their witness of courage can make a big difference both inside and outside the youth group. I call this last big spiritual step to be taken during the high school youth group years the "take a stand in the world" step.

Saint Paul's second letter coaching young Timothy as he went forth into his ministry has the same kind of encouraging tone our seniors need from us as they go forth: "I am reminding you now to fan into a flame the gift of God that you possess

through the laying on of my hands. God did not give us a spirit of timidity, but the Spirit of power and love and self-control" (2 Tim. 1:6–7, NJB).

Summary

Now I will summarize in single words the spiritual break-through possible in each year of a high school youth group journey. The words are *openness, faith, influence,* and *courage.* These fine human qualities are latent in everyone, but they can easily remain buried without a strong spiritual context to call them forth. In a Christ-centered youth group they grow quite normally, illustrating in gradual stages Saint Paul's words, "If any one is in Christ, he is a new creation . . ." (2 Cor. 5:17, RSV).

   In the diagram that follows, I depict the four aspects of my schema. The typical concerns of each grade level are shown as zones the young people enter. The spiritual challenges we offer are shown as messages addressed to the young people at each zone. And the growth steps of openness, faith, influence, and courage are shown as stairs descending into greater depth of person. The movement is different from the usual patterns of adolescent development that focus primarily on the development of adult coping skills. Here another dimension is added. The maturing Christian is learning to walk on the solid ground of realized Gospel values and, from that footing, will learn to master life's external circumstances.

Challenge we offer	"Be yourself with others."	"Be your best with Christ."	"Take charge in the group."	"Take a stand in the world."
Growth step	Openness			
		Faith		
			Influence	
				Courage
Developmental need	Acceptance	Recognition	Values Decisions	Moving On
Grade level	Freshmen	Sophomores	Juniors	Seniors

Acknowledgments (*continued*)

The scriptural quotations cited as NIV are taken from the Holy Bible, New International Version. Copyright © 1973, 1978, 1984 by the International Bible Society. Used with permission of Zondervan Bible Publishers and Hodder and Stoughton Publishers. All rights reserved.

The scriptural quotations cited as NJB are taken from the New Jerusalem Bible. Copyright © 1985 by Darton, Longman and Todd, and Doubleday, a division of Bantam, Doubleday, Dell Publishing Group. Reprinted with permission of the publishers.

The scriptural quotations cited as RSV are taken from the Revised Standard Version. Copyright © 1946, 1956, 1971 by the Division of Christian Education of the National Council of the Churches of Christ in the United States of America. Used with permission.

Chapters 1–7 and 16–22 are articles written by Robert Doolittle that originally appeared in the *Pilot,* the official publication of the Archdiocese of Boston.

The material on the five stages of dealing with loss on pages 64–66 is adapted from *On Death and Dying,* by Elisabeth Kübler-Ross (New York: Macmillan, 1969), pages 148–159. Copyright © 1969 by Elisabeth Kübler-Ross. Adapted with permission of Macmillan Publishing Co. and Travistock Publications.

The Wink game on page 25 is adapted from *More New Games* (New York: Doubleday, 1981), page 109. Copyright © 1981 by the Headlands Press. Used with permission of Doubleday, a division of Bantam, Doubleday, Dell Publishing Group.

What Others Are Saying . . .

"In this two-part series, Bob Doolittle, a seasoned and committed coordinator of youth ministry, offers excellent ideas and ways of doing youth ministry that are practical, creative, challenging, scripturally oriented, and Christ-centered. His books show an obvious love of and dedication to youth and are a valuable resource for parish youth ministers." **Rev. Richard L. Harrington**, director, Office of Youth Ministry, Archdiocese of Boston

"This two-volume series provides the reader with an excellent resource in responding to issues of youth ministry in the areas of youth-led planning, developing peer leaders, gaining parental support, developing inquiring minds, and much more. The premise of Catholic Christian development and training are evident throughout the texts. This series provides a beneficial resource for the new youth minister as well as the seasoned youth minister." **Linda Campbell, OSB**, director, Diocese of Phoenix, and chair, National Federation for Catholic Youth Ministry

"Whether you are just starting out or are a seasoned veteran in youth ministry, you will find Bob Doolittle's two-volume series an invaluable resource. His blend of practical ideas with philosophical, theological insights are clearly and creatively presented and are borne out of years of field-tested experience and the author's longstanding love for Christ, the Church, and young people. These books will raise your vision, encourage you, and give you plenty of useful ideas for ministry to young people." **Jack Carpenter**, Young Life New England, thirty-year youth ministry professional